How to READ a Balance Sheet

Rick J. Makoujy, Jr.

New York   Chicago   San Francisco   Lisbon   London
Madrid   Mexico City   Milan   New Delhi   San Juan
Seoul   Singapore   Sydney   Toronto

1 2 3 4 5 6 7 8 9 10   WFR/WFR   1 5 4 3 2 1 0

ISBN   978-0-07-170033-7
MHID   0-07-170033-1

This publication is designed to provide accurate and authoritative information in regard to the subject matter covered. It is sold with the understanding that neither the author nor the publisher is engaged in rendering legal, accounting, futures/securities trading, or other professional service. If legal advice or other expert assistance is required, the services of a competent professional person should be sought.

> —*From a Declaration of Principles jointly adopted*
> *by a Committee of the American Bar Association*
> *and a Committee of Publishers*

McGraw-Hill books are available at special quantity discounts to use as premiums and sales promotions or for use in corporate training programs. To contact a representative, please e-mail us at bulksales@mcgraw-hill.com.

CONTENTS

Contents

PREFACE

Don't be afraid of this book. My intention is to explain financial statements and related concepts in easy-to-understand language, not confusing industry jargon as is found in every other finance-related work I've seen. The goal is to impart solid comprehension. If you can't do so already, after carefully reading this book you will be able to understand the business section of any newspaper, including my favorite, *The Wall Street Journal*. You will also find that while that the skills and knowledge described herein are business oriented, there are also parallels throughout this book to one's personal financial well-being.

. . .

The genesis of this book is, as Paul McCartney and John Lennon (mostly McCartney), so eloquently put it, a "Long and Winding Road," but which may be succinctly summarized as *accounting is taught wrong*. While I scraped by with a "B" in Accounting 101 as an undergraduate at Vanderbilt University, I walked away from the course feeling slightly less educated than I was before the class started. It seemed as though the professor received satisfaction from tricking the students. "Sooo," she would say while pointing to the board wearing a Cheshire cat grin, "Is it a debit or a credit?" Most of the class would sheepishly state in nervous whispers, "Debit"? "*No!*" she would thunder. "It's a *credit*! Ha, ha, ha!"

I learned much later that she was, in effect, teaching us a little bit of brain surgery. Unless her students were likely to be accounting professionals in some capacity, general ledger entries and debits and credits only serve to confuse the bigger picture (which, frankly, is all that most people will ever need but few will ever properly understand).

After college, I landed a job with Price Waterhouse's (PW) Restructuring Practice in New York City. We helped those who were owed money (i.e., creditors) from companies in bankruptcy (i.e., debtors) figure out what they might ultimately recover as a percentage of what they were owed. As a junior professional, my job was to input data and create many spreadsheets. (I became a Lotus 1–2–3 wiz.) Despite PW's status of being a premier "Big Six" accounting firm (alongside Coopers & Lybrand, which later merged with PW; Arthur Anderson, which later imploded during the Enron document shredding scandal; Deloitte & Touche; Ernst & Young; and KPMG Peat Marwick), I really wasn't close to being proficient in accounting, even after a couple of years. My salary seemed generous on the surface until I moved New York City, absorbed the much higher cost of living, and divided my income by the hours worked.

Two years later, anxious to move past paycheck-to-paycheck living, I solicited various Wall Street firms for open positions. Fortunately, the Price Waterhouse name on my résumé opened interview doors; I landed a job as a securities analyst for a distressed securities broker-age firm that had broken off from Bear Stearns. (Remember them?) The firm was relatively small and had no formal training program but assumed that my skills were far more advanced than they were. I was asked on my first day to create projected balance sheets for a company in bankruptcy protection. I had no clue as to what to do. Fearful of losing the job I so badly needed, I sat down with an annual report and my trusty Lotus 1–2–3 spreadsheets.

Starting with the relatively straightforward income statement, I figured out the simple subtraction to get from revenue to net income. However, the interaction between the statements proved to be more of a challenge. If net income increased, shouldn't cash on the balance sheet go up by the same amount? After some contemplation, it occurred to me that, for example, if a company had recorded a sale but had not yet gotten paid, its receivables (money owed by customers) would go up. This increase in receivables, while still counted as part of net income, would not increase cash until the customers paid their bills. Making similar adjustments for increases in equipment purchases and borrowings, I finally got the result I so desperately sought: the balance sheet balanced. In other words, the company's assets equaled its liabilities plus net worth. My first reaction was relief and joy. My second was: Why hadn't anyone ever explained financial statements to me like this before? Career lightbulb no.1 went on.

Over the next couple of years, I became proficient at securities analysis and breathed much more easily knowing that my job was secure. I became partner and helped form a corporate finance division (we helped find investors for companies or projects) within our organization. Two of the projects for which we raised capital were struggling: an insurance company based in Bermuda that we had purchased from the Travelers Group and a company I founded in Texas for the purpose of recycling, or scrapping, the U.S. Navy's vast fleet of "mothballed" ships. The investor groups in both cases asked me and two partners to take over the management of each firm. We left the company, formed our own, and rolled up our sleeves. The insurance company's costs were slashed, and investment revenue jumped as we diversified its investment portfolio. The firm was ultimately sold to a much larger insurance company at a substantial profit to the investor group.

The ship-breaking firm, however, was hit hard by the Asian crisis of the late 1990s. In an effort to raise "hard" currency, steel producers in Russia, China, and elsewhere started "dumping" their finished steel products in the United States. The prices they sought for the steel were so low that domestic steel producers actually shut down their mills in many cases, instead of filling their customer orders through the purchase and resale of the cheap Asian imports. Unfortunately, there aren't many uses for scrap steel other than melting it to make new steel products. Due to its weight, scrap is also very costly to transport. Consequently, since the primary source of revenue for a ship-scrapping concern is the sale of scrap metal, operating results took a nosedive as scrap prices plummeted from about $160 per ton to around $60 per ton in fewer than 60 days.

Times were tough, especially since we as principals had personally guaranteed millions of dollars of debt obligations to help fund the company's development. In addition, we were having trouble collecting money from our customers as the steel production industry was struggling. In other words, even though we were supposedly selling enough product to pay our bills (barely), there was insufficient cash available to pay payroll, lease expenses, and so on. Our receivables were growing; this was effectively a painful use of cash. The second career lightbulb was illuminated. The theoretical lesson about receivables growth "using" cash learned years earlier on paper was now being put to actual use. We had to dip into our pockets repeatedly to avoid the catastrophe associated with missing payroll and defaulting on the huge debt obligations.

We made it through. Though the process was painful, we found a financial partner willing to put up additional capital. Government contracts and commodity price improvement allowed the company to work through a difficult time. Once the business stabilized, I left my partners in order to venture out on my own, wiser for the experience.

Over the next few years, I undertook many ventures, including buying, "fixing," and selling about 10 companies and 60 real estate projects, and performing turnaround consulting for troubled businesses. More and more, I was becoming a resource for others seeking financial and operational guidance. One day, a close friend at a very high level position at a Fortune 500 company called me, frantically seeking "secret" advice regarding a meeting he was to attend the next day. His employer was considering acquiring a smaller company, and the meeting was intended to evaluate the merits of such a pursuit. "What does accretive mean?" he asked. "And what is EBITDA?" Happy to help, I took the time to chat with him and explained clearly what he needed to know. Gratefully, he responded by offering me a generous compliment: "I always thought accounting was so complicated," he shared. "You make it seem so simple." "That's because accounting is taught wrong," I contended. "I could teach you accounting in an hour." "You can't teach accounting in an hour!" he exclaimed. "Sure I can," was my reply. "Then you're hired!" he shouted. "Our executives desperately need financial literacy but can't spare much time."

So with my proverbial foot in my mouth, I wrote a course and gave the presentation, titled "Accounting In An Hour," which was extremely well received. Since accounting had become a hot topic with the implosion of Enron, WorldCom, Sunbeam, and others, I decided to put out feelers to assess the potential market reaction to my 60-minute lecture.

Huge. Many companies were seeking just such a solution. Now my career had taken an unexpected turn—training others. I traveled around giving the seminar to large organizations and met with the training folks at Goldman Sachs. Goldman loved the idea and offered to purchase the program "If you put it online—our people are scattered all over the place." Not knowing anything about e-learning but wanting Goldman's cash, I assembled a top team to modify my plain PowerPoint presentation into a snappy online and DVD-based financial literacy training tool. Suddenly, the instructor-led lecture had become an extremely well received e-learning platform. The company, In An Hour, LLC, has been approached by several publishers about the creation of a modern-day "For Dummies" series under the In An Hour—Get Smarter Faster brand. The Best Practice Institute has labeled me "one of the top experts in the world," and McGraw-Hill has asked me to write this book for you.

Normally, I enjoy providing operational and financial guidance to troubled institutions, both public and private. There is an inherent satisfaction to seeing the lessons I've learned benefiting others. And there are a few more books rattling around in my head. Let's see what you think of this one first. . . . .

ACKNOWLEDGMENTS

This book is dedicated to my loving family. I have been very fortunate to have a supportive and understanding wife who has accepted my non-traditional (and sometimes volatile) career path. We have gone through countless difficult situations over the last 15 years. She recognizes, however, that I possess an entrepreneur's spirit, and she is able to focus on our many successes along the way. If it weren't for Jackie, I'd be working a nine to five (or more likely a seven to ten) job and wouldn't be writing this book for you.

My children, Aristotle and Sloan Falcon, are my inspiration. I couldn't be prouder of my two smart, funny, and athletic boys. When all is said and done, it is their excellent well-being that is my ultimate source of joy. I recently watched (and heard) six-year old Aristotle break his leg wrestling a far larger opponent. His toughness through the pain and desire to continue wrestling this season humble me. Four months after being in a wheelchair, he took first place in a major wrestling tournament. Amazing!

My parents provided a stable environment for me and my sister Caroline growing up and offered us great educational opportunities. Their sacrifices and support along the way are also greatly appreciated.

I've been fortunate to have had the opportunity to experience many business adventures. I hope that the lessons learned along the way will offer you a quicker and easier path to the knowledge absorbed (sometimes painfully) along the way.

And thank you, the reader, for taking the time to read on. I understand how scarce the resource has become over the last few years.

INTRODUCTION

Remember WorldCom, later renamed MCI? The telecommunications giant, along with its investors, suffered a terrible fate due to a systematic failure to adhere to the guidance contained in this book. A recurring theme herein will be the practice of recognizing that an expense occurs when value is lost. WorldCom inappropriately failed to make such acknowledgments to the tune of $11 billion, resulting in one of the largest corporate scandals in history. Instead of justly expensing the $11 billion of lost value, the company took the position that it had added substantial assets to its balance sheet from 1999 through 2002. This process resulted in artificial profits and had the effect of unfairly propping up the company's share price. When the fictitious asset values were ultimately discovered, WorldCom filed for bankruptcy protection, causing tens of billions of dollars of investor losses. Bernard Ebbers, its chief executive officer, was sent to prison to serve a 25-year sentence at Oakdale Federal Correctional Complex in Louisiana.

I'm writing this book because I find the extent to which financial literacy is lacking in our society deplorable. Many small business owners or employees in large organizations are responsible for decisions that directly impact the bottom line. Unfortunately, their lack of basic accounting and finance knowledge leads to tremendous operational inefficiencies. As the global economy becomes increasingly competitive, inappropriately motivated choices cause companies to suffer, leading to loan defaults and job losses.

Culled from a wild adventure of a career, during which many of these lessons were learned the hard way, you'll garner and retain more practical—and valuable—information from this book than from any other you have read. My goal is to empower you through improved knowledge and resultant heightened confidence and superior decision making.

In order to lay a foundation for increasingly complex topics, I'll begin with a short summary of the two important financial statements: the income statement and balance sheet. An income statement shows how much money has been brought into an organization, how much is spent, and how much, if any, is left over: revenue minus expenses equals profit (or loss) *over a period of time*. A balance sheet is a snapshot of what a business owns, how much it owes, and what is left over: assets minus liabilities equals equity (or net worth) *at a specific point in time*. While the focus of this book deals with the balance sheet and peripheral issues, the concepts of the income statement and the balance sheet are interrelated and must be examined in conjunction with each other. One must understand not only what a business or individual possesses and owes at year end but also how much is earned or lost over time.

I'll then provide a more comprehensive view of the balance sheet, breaking it down into its various components. The different types of short-term, or current, assets such as cash, inventory, accounts receivable, and prepaid expenses (things expected to be turned into cash or used as cash within a year from the date of the balance sheet) will be explained in more detail. Long-term assets, or possessions, including equipment, furniture, and real estate, which are used to operate a business (and are not expected to be sold within 12 months) will then be examined.

The book will next describe the various forms of obligations a company might have incurred. Short-term, or current, liabilities are those debts that must be paid within a year. Examples of current liabilities include accounts payable, accrued expenses, and that portion of long-term debt that comes due over the next 12 months. Next, we'll look at longer-term IOUs, which needn't be paid for at least a year. Long-term liabilities include equipment loans, real estate mortgages, and bond liabilities.

As mentioned, the difference between assets and liabilities is called "net worth," or equity. Equity can consist of several forms. Paid-in capital is the money contributed to a company by its owners. Retained earnings are the accumulated profits that a business has generated over time. Additionally, equity often consists of multiple tranches. Preferred stock is senior to common stock, much like a first mortgage has priority over a second mortgage on a building. There are different forms of preferred stock, just as there are numerous varieties of common equity. Depending on the type of business or organization, owners might possess membership interests, common shares, or partnership percentages. All equity holders, regardless of type, are junior in right of payment to liabilities.

Once I've laid the basic groundwork of financial literacy through the explanation of the income statement and balance sheet, I'll move on to cover applications of this knowledge. The first such subject will be the differences between cash-based accounting and accrual-based accounting. Cash-based accounting simply records transactions when money is received or paid. The more accurate accrual-based method keeps track of when liabilities are incurred or assets are recorded, regardless of whether cash transfers have occurred yet.

Additional topics will include the valuation of inventory, or goods on hand for sale. When a business purchases identical products at different prices for resale to customers, it may choose which to "sell" first. LIFO, or last in, first out, is the process by which the most recently acquired identical product is identified as the one sold. FIFO, or first in, first out, on the other hand, suggests that the oldest identical product in inventory is the one disposed of first. Deciding which of the two methodologies to utilize may have a significant impact on the timing of a company's profitability.

Another major challenge faced by many organizations is the management of working capital. In other words, how much short-term cash is available to a business to purchase inventory and meet the needs of its current liabilities as well as other ongoing requirements? Many companies, especially small ones, find this task daunting. I describe the challenge and offer several solutions. Vendor financing, receivables factoring, and quick pay discounts are three of the answers provided. Each offers a way for organizations to better align cash receipts and necessary payments.

The next issue tackled is the frequent discrepancy between the carrying value of an organization's assets on the balance sheet and their actual market value. While assets are originally listed on a company's books at their original cost, several factors cause the asset values to fluctuate, even while the book values remain relatively constant. The way to account for a gradual loss in value of a long-term asset over its estimated useful life is called "depreciation" for tangible assets, which we may touch and feel. The slow decline in the book value of intangible assets (those that we can't touch or feel, like patents or developed technology) is deemed "amortization." Depreciation and amortization can significantly reduce a company's future profitability without the associated cash costs. There are many ways that a business may choose to account for the gradual loss of value of these long-term assets. I'll discuss several in some detail.

Sometimes, asset values drop precipitously in a short time frame, such as when a customer that owes you money files for bankruptcy or when a product development failure occurs. In these cases, the book, or carrying, value of the impaired asset may be rapidly adjusted downward in a process known as a write-down. When the write-down eliminates all of the value of the asset (now deemed to be worthless), the exercise is considered a write-off.

The next subject I describe is the difference between operating leases and capital leases. Companies require assets necessary for the operation of their business, such as equipment. The structure of the agreement utilized to acquire these items varies but has a significant impact on each organization's balance sheet and income statement. The pros and cons of each variety are explained.

Some companies seeking liquidity must raise money through borrowing funds, diluting existing owners through equity sales or are forced to sell assets on their balance sheets. Investors sometimes purchase these items and then effectively rent them back to the company for a negotiated rate of interest. Deemed "sale leaseback transactions," such maneuvers may be viewed as a sign of financial weakness, which requires the ostensible borrower to transfer ownership of the underlying asset. I will describe this process.

Another covered topic that is widely used in financial statement preparation, asset valuations, and business purchases is net present value. Net present value, or NPV, determines the present worth of a future earnings stream. In this fashion, appropriate pricing may be established to determine whether or not certain asset acquisitions make sense. NPV is an important tool in financial statement analysis.

Capital expenditures (or CapEx, for short) are the regular purchases of assets necessary to operate a business. Tools and machinery, for example, must be relatively new and/or properly updated to preserve operating efficiency to keep a company competitive. These important monetary outlays are often overlooked by overly optimistic investors as a required use of future cash. I will explain the importance of CapEx as a balance sheet adjustment despite its lack of immediate impact on the income statement.

Our next agenda item is cash flow. Loosely speaking, cash flow is supposed to represent the amount of money a business can generate over a period of time. Unfortunately, cash flow is defined differently by many different constituencies, and many of them interpret the concept incorrectly. I will set the record straight.

When an organization is unable to honor its obligations and defaults on its debts, it is often forced to file for bankruptcy. In this case, those liabilities that don't have specific and sufficient collateral to ensure repayment become subject to compromise. Liabilities subject to compromise generally don't recover anywhere near the amount of their claim against the debtor. The text will describe this process.

Sometimes liabilities for which a company may be obligated are dependent on outside circumstances. An example of these contingent liabilities is a pending lawsuit. Should the business lose the case, it might be on the hook for a substantial sum. But how would a company account for such an eventuality on its balance sheet? I will share the rationale and implementation of this procedure as well as its applicability to public institutions.

Once the aforementioned topics have been laid out, we'll then move on to balance sheet analysis. In short, does it look okay? What red flags should an investor or vendor look for when considering the extension of credit or investment of capital to an enterprise? The first consideration discussed is asset quality. Are the items listed worth their stated book values? How can one tell?

One analysis tool covered herein is the monitoring of accounts payable. Often the last to be paid, a growth in obligations to vendors relative to sales may be an early warning sign that a business may be experiencing financial distress.

Fiscal problems often manifest themselves in other forms as well. A company that is having trouble raising money might be forced to give up ownership of its assets to an effective lender. These sale leaseback arrangements call for a business to liquidate assets, often at discounted prices and then pay for the future use of the items that are no longer owned. These structures, currently in use by the State of California and American Airlines, protect investors from distressed borrowers by granting them immediate ownership in (generally) tangible assets, skipping the otherwise necessary foreclosure process should a loan default occur.

I'll then explain how corporate executives are, in effect, fund managers, working on behalf of company owners. Unlike mutual funds, business managers use different tools. Instead of using cash to buy stocks or bonds, they have equipment, real estate, accounts receivable, inventory, and employees to manage. Their job performance may be measured by how well they are able to generate profits for the company's owners using those assets relative to other managers within the same industry, deemed to be a "return on assets test." Return on equity is a similar measure of executive skill that also factors in the use of borrowings to improve (at least theoretically) profitability to shareholders in the company.

The debt-to-equity ratio is a measurement of financial risk that is determined by how much a business borrows (and is obligated to repay) relative to the amount of capital the company has raised through owner contributions or retained profits. Beware of companies that are overly reliant on debt; performance hiccups may have a devastating effect on company viability.

Another way we may monitor financial statement vulnerability is through an audit process. An audit is the process by which an "independent" accounting firm reviews and opines on a company's income statement and balance sheet and the ways by which they have been created. While an audit generally requires only spot-checking, it often uncovers inconsistencies, which may then prompt further investigation. Some audits have led to ultimate fiscal collapse of large businesses once it has been revealed that mistakes or outright improprieties have been masking poor performance.

Balance sheet changes should also be considered when business performance is examined. A business that is unable to collect from its customers on a timely basis or needs to increase borrowings to survive without revenue growth ultimately may be a candidate for bankruptcy. Some of these modifications, coupled with details about preparation methods of the financial statement, specific debt due dates, available credit lines, and an auditor opinion letter, are described in the notes to a company's financial statements. These notes must be reviewed carefully by an investor in conjunction with the statements themselves to derive a more complete understanding of a corporation's fiscal well-being.

Once I've described the income statement and balance sheet, coupled with other basic analysis tools, I'll move on to ways in which a balance sheet may be utilized to maximize value for company owners. One such process is the use of a company's equity as currency. A corporation might preserve cash by using shares of stock to reward employees, reduce debt, or acquire assets, including other businesses. The measurement of how well management executes this is a function of whether or not the profit allocation to each piece of ownership grows or shrinks due to such moves. Equity transactions that increase earnings per share are deemed accretive, and they therefore are desirable. On the other hand, when equity is used as currency and earnings per share decline as a result, the process is considered dilutive.

Other covered topics will include the impact of inflation and currency fluctuations on the balance sheet and the income statement.

It is important to understand how these uncontrollable factors affect a company's fiscal fortunes. This understanding also aids in preparing for such eventualities should managers or outside investors seek to hedge against either occurrence.

We'll then segue into causes of the recent financial meltdowns. We begin with a description of the era of easy money, describing how cheap debt (very low interest rates to sometimes dubious borrowers) resulted in tremendous overleveraging by individuals and businesses alike. This process was fueled by poor public policy decisions, dubious analysis by rating agencies, and greed. A government philosophy that home ownership was a right, not a privilege, forced financial institutions to make questionable loans to unqualified borrowers. These loans were then packaged and sold in bundles to Wall Street institutions and other investors, aided by overly optimistic assessments by rating agencies. The ultimate result was a seizure of the global economy's financial system and trillions of dollars of losses.

The avoidance of such situations is our next topic. Managing risk and protecting assets may reduce the likelihood of repeated home runs but mitigates the chance of disaster. Examples of how this may be accomplished include diversification, strong management, minimal debt usage, insurance in various forms, and asset sheltering. Instead if home runs, we'll take singles and doubles (and sleep soundly) all day long.

You may have heard that the cash flow statement is the third important financial statement. This is false. While I'll describe how it works, it is important to note that the cash flow statement provides no new information (provided that the balance sheets have sufficient detail). It simply illustrates balance sheet changes to show the sources and uses of cash balances. For this reason, I devote only a relatively modest portion of the book to the cash flow statement.

To put this newfound wisdom to use, I will next outline common mistakes entrepreneurs make when starting a business (and how to avoid such pitfalls) and how management skills may be improved through heightened financial literacy. I'll walk you through the steps necessary to ensure your success, whether you're a manager of a part of a larger organization or an owner of a more modest business. In either case, you need to maximize profits for the company's owners through effective management of the assets under your direction (including employees, which require cash). The necessary tools for either role are essentially the same.

Lastly, I'll summarize the most important elements covered in the book in order to facilitate retention. Don't be afraid to keep the book handy as a reference guide!

I'm very proud of the amount and quality of knowledge condensed in this book. I hope you find it to be a valuable shortcut to information culled from many years of experiences. Happy reading!

1

PRIMER ON THE BALANCE SHEET AND INCOME STATEMENT

WHAT IS A BALANCE SHEET?

The good news is that reading financial statements is easy. Let's start with a short overview of the first of two important financial statements, the balance sheet.

> **The balance sheet shows what a company's assets are (what it owns), what its liabilities are (what it owes), and what its equity is (what's left over) at a specific point in time.**

That's it. Memorize that sentence—it's pretty important. By the way, the specific point in time is usually the end of the year or the end of a quarter. Simplistically, what did I *own* and what did I *owe* at the end of last year, and what was the difference between the two?

To start, there are three principal components of a balance sheet. The first, assets, is things that are owned. There are many types of assets. Assets that are readily converted into or used as cash are deemed short term in nature. Examples of short-term, or current, assets are cash, monies due from customers (called "accounts receivable"), inventory (stocked items for sale), or any other owned items that are expected to be liquidated or used as cash within one year from the date on the balance sheet.

Assets such as real estate, furniture, or equipment used to operate the business are generally not expected to be sold within 12 months. Consequently, these owned items are classified as long term in nature. Long-term assets maintain their value over an extended time frame based on their estimated useful lives. A building, for example, will not decline in value as quickly as a computer, and less of its cost is lost each year as a result.

On the other side of the ledger, a company that owns assets typically also owes money to various people or entities in the form of liabilities. Liabilities are simply IOUs. A business or individual might owe money to employees in the form of accrued payroll or vacation time, to vendors (suppliers who have shipped product or provided services with the expectation of payment in 30 or 60 days, called "accounts payable"), to banks in the form of credit cards or other debt, to the Internal Revenue Service, or to other creditors. Those debts that must be paid within a year from the balance sheet's date are considered short-term liabilities. Obligations that needn't be paid for at least 12 months are deemed long-term liabilities.

The difference between assets and liabilities is called "net worth," or equity. In short, if you were to sell the assets shown on a balance sheet at their listed values and use the proceeds to pay off the stated liabilities, whatever is left would be considered equity. Equity is the value the owners have in the business. Similarly, an individual might sell his or her possessions, satisfy all creditors with the proceeds, and keep whatever is left over for himself or herself. Keep in mind that it is possible to have negative equity if the proposed asset sales wouldn't result in enough cash to pay off the listed liabilities.

Let's look at an easy example. Imagine buying a house for $100,000, with a $10,000 down payment and a $90,000 mortgage. You've just created a balance sheet. A $100,000 asset (the house) equals the $90,000 liability (the mortgage) plus $10,000 in equity (also called "net worth"). In other words, if you sell the asset and use the proceeds to pay off the liabilities, you get net worth, or equity.

Of course, companies (and individuals) have assets of varying kinds in addition to real estate. These include cash, inventory, equipment, and patents. We owe money in forms other than mortgages, such as taxes, utility bills, credit cards, and payroll. Net worth, or equity, is calculated by subtracting total liabilities from total assets. It's simple.

PRIMER ON THE INCOME STATEMENT

To fully understand the balance sheet, you need to be familiar with another major financial statement, the income statement (also called the "P&L," or "profit and loss statement"). Here's an overview.

The income statement (P&L) shows how much money a company generates, how much it spends, and what is left over during a period of time.

Easy. By the way, the income statement's period of time is often one year or one calendar quarter. I'll illustrate the income statement through the use of a simple example: Jackie's Hardware Store.

The first component of the income statement is revenue. Revenue is the money an organization receives before paying any expenses. Sales are the portion of revenue that comes from selling products or services to customers, such as retailers getting money for stocked goods, or legal fees paid to an attorney. Other sources of revenue include proceeds from a tenant's rent to a landlord or royalties received by an author from a publisher.

For nonprofit organizations, annual revenue may be referred to as "gross receipts" and may come from donations from individual or corporate donors, fund-raising, membership dues, grants from government agencies, or return on investments. Tax revenue is money that a government receives from taxpayers. In many countries, including the United Kingdom, revenue is called "turnover."

The price of goods or services multiplied by the number of those items sold determines a company's annual revenue. In Jackie's Hardware Store, Jackie receives money from selling products like hammers, saws, and nails to her customers. Let's imagine that she sold 1,000 hammers last year for $10 each. She would have generated $10,000 in hammer revenue. Similarly, she sold 2,000 saws last year for $20 each, creating $40,000 in saw revenue. If we add the total revenue from hammers and saws to the revenue from all of the other products in her store last year, we'll assume that she generated $1 million in total revenue, which in her case comes from sales.

Hammers	$ 1,000
Price Each	× $ 10
Hammer Revenue	$10,000

Saws		2,000
Price Each	× $	20
Saw Revenue	$	40,000
Hammer Revenue	$	10,000
Other Sales	+ $	950,000
Total Revenue		$1,000,000

The next piece of the income statement is direct costs. Direct costs are those expenses that are directly correlated with sales. In other words, if Jackie generates zero revenue, theoretically, her direct costs should also be zero. Examples of direct costs are commissions (which are paid only when sales occur) and the cost of the goods that she sells. Jackie does not have any commissioned salespeople in her store, so her only direct costs are from the products that she sells.

It is important to note that the purchase of inventory is not an expense when Jackie buys the goods. This transaction is simply the transfer of one asset, cash, to another asset, inventory. The expense occurs when *the value is lost*. When the hammer becomes someone else's property and the customer walks out of the store, Jackie's Hardware Store no longer owns it. The value is lost at the time of the sale. The recording of the sale (generation of revenue) occurs simultaneously with the expensing of the inventory even though it was previously purchased.

Last year, as we learned, Jackie sold 1,000 hammers. Her cost per hammer was $5 each, so her direct cost associated with the sale of hammers was $5,000. Her cost per saw was $10 each, so her direct costs for saws last year on the 2,000 that she sold was $20,000. Let's add her direct costs for hammers to her direct costs for saws to all of her other direct costs last year. We'll suppose that she had total direct costs for the year of $500,000. For example:

Direct Costs	
Commissioned salespeople	$ 0
Cost of goods	
Hammers	$ 5,000
Saws	20,000
Other Cost of Goods	475,000
Total Direct Costs	$500,000

Subtracting direct costs from revenue yields gross profit. Jackie's gross profit last year can be simply calculated as $1,000,000 of revenue less $500,000 of direct costs equals $500,000 of gross profit:

Revenue	$1,000,000
Direct Costs	−500,000
Gross Profit	$ 500,000

Her gross margin is $500,000 of gross profit divided by total revenue of $1,000,000, or 50 percent:

$$\$500,000 \div \$1,000,000 = 0.50$$

or 50% gross margin

In other words, half of her revenue goes to purchase the items she sells, her inventory. Obviously, the higher the gross profit, the better. If a company has a negative gross profit because its sales don't even cover the cost of goods that are sold, it might as well close its doors, as there is no money left over to fund the other expenses the business has to incur.

Different types of businesses have vastly differing gross margins. A software company (e.g., Microsoft) that creates a program (e.g., Microsoft Office) once may sell it many, many times. Once the code is written, the cost of burning a disk and putting it into a box is trivial relative to the purchase price of a couple of hundred dollars. Obviously, the more copies that are sold, the easier it will be to absorb the cost of content creation over a larger customer base.

Grocery stores, on the other hand, have notoriously low gross margins. Many items are sold below cost as "loss leaders" to induce customers to enter the store. Some food, such as fruit and vegetables, dairy products, bread products, and meat and chicken or seafood, is perishable and is thrown away regularly because realistically it is never completely sold. Due to the slim gross margins under which these companies must operate, it is imperative that they sell large volumes of products in order to generate sufficient gross profit to cover operating expenses (see below).

Generally speaking, when a company is able to raise prices, few of its expenses increase in tandem. Increasing revenue through higher prices to customers usually has a substantially beneficial impact on gross margin and gross profit. Conversely, when competitive pressures require discounting to retain customers and associated sales, gross margin and gross profit suffer.

Operating expenses are those costs that are incurred regardless of revenue generation. Examples are rent, noncommissioned payroll, health insurance premiums, utility bills, and real estate taxes. Operating expenses are sometimes referred to as "overhead." In Jackie's case, her operating expenses last year consisted of $120,000 of noncommissioned payroll, $20,000 of advertising and promotion, $10,000 of utilities,

$10,000 of insurance premiums, and $140,000 of other operating expenses, for a total of $300,000 in operating expenses:

Operating Expenses	
Payroll	$120,000
Advertising and Promotion	20,000
Utilities	10,000
Insurance	10,000
Other Operating Expenses	140,000
Total Operating Expenses	$300,000

Operating profit is simply the difference between gross profit and operating expenses. Fortunately, in Jackie's case, her gross profit of $500,000 was more than sufficient to cover her operating expenses of $300,000, leaving her with an operating profit of $200,000.

Operating profit divided by revenue is operating margin. Jackie's operating margin last year was $200,000 divided by $1,000,000, or 20 percent. Operating profit is an indicator of how much money a business generates after paying its regular costs to operate. This figure helps business buyers or lenders understand how much money is left over to pay debt service, to provide a return to the owners of the company, or both.

Reaching breakeven at the operating profit level is an important milestone for a business. Once administrative costs and overhead are effectively paid for, incremental gross profit flows through to the operating income level (provided that the extra revenue does not warrant additional staff). You likely don't need another accountant or receptionist with higher sales. Nor would you need to rent another facility or increase utility costs. For this reason, a company that is able to "cover its nut" with existing revenue may take on more customers, even if those sales are less profitable. Every additional dollar of gross profit flows through to operating profit at that point, adding value to the business.

It is from operating profit that Jackie must pay nonoperating expenses, such as interest and taxes. Jackie's only interest-bearing obligation is the $900,000 mortgage on her building. This mortgage bears interest at 10 percent per year. Her interest expense, consequently, was $90,000 last year (simply calculated as mortgage balance of $900,000 times the interest rate of 10 percent). Subtracting her interest expense of $90,000 from her operating profit of $200,000 left her with pretax income of $110,000 for the 12-month period.

The government's only concession to a business's success is to tax income after expenses are deducted. Assuming a 30 percent tax bite, Jackie's Hardware Store had a $33,000 tax obligation last year [calculated simply as pretax income of $110,000 times 0.30 (a tax rate of 30 percent)]. Subtracting the $33,000 tax amount from her $110,000 pretax income left her with $77,000 of net income last year.

Net income is simply operating profit less any nonoperating expenses, such as interest, taxes, or losses on stocks. Here are the calculations for Jackie's Hardware Store:

Revenue	$1,000,000
Direct Costs	−500,000
Gross Profit	$ 500,000
Operating Expenses	−300,000
Operating Profit	$ 200,000
Interest Expense	−90,000
Pretax Income	$ 110,000
Taxes	−33,000
Net Profit (or Loss)	$ 77,000

Interest can be either an expense or a source of income. If a business borrows money, the cost of doing so is deemed interest expense and is deducted from pretax income. On the other hand, a company that maintains cash balances that generate interest income would add this amount to pretax income. A blend of the two (some interest-bearing cash or short-term investments along with a number of obligations requiring interest payments) are often combined in a net interest expense or net interest income figure on the income statement.

For example, if a company had $1 million in cash and short-term investments last year, which provided 5 percent interest, the firm would have received $50,000 in interest income. During the same period, a $2 million equipment loan cost the company 8 percent interest. This $160,000 interest expense ($2,000,000 times 8 percent) would more than exceed the interest income. The net interest expense figure recorded by the business would have been $110,000, calculated simply as $160,000 in interest expense less the $50,000 of interest income generated.

Taxes suck. The monies that constitute aggregate pretax income are subject to income taxes. (If you have negative pretax income, you wouldn't have the obligation.) Income taxes are based on the state in which the business is based, the level of pretax income generated, and the type of business organization involved. C corporations (more on company types in Chapter 4), for example, pay income tax on pretax income. S corporations, partnerships, and limited liability companies generally do not pay income taxes. Instead, S corporations, partnerships, and limited liability companies' pretax income is "passed through" to the owners in their pro rata ownership percentages. An S corporation with $1 million of pretax income that has four individual equal shareholders (owners) would allocate this pretax income to the owners. The $250,000 each shareholder would be assessed would obligate the owners to assume the responsibility for the taxes due on their profit share, regardless of whether or not any distributions were made to help cover the cost of the tax. If no distributions are made in this case and the shareholders had to pay their share of taxes due, the allocated pretax income would be called "phantom income."

Payroll taxes and collected sales taxes are not lumped in with nonoperating expenses like income taxes. Payroll taxes and sales taxes are considered operating or direct expenses. Payroll taxes on direct expense employees like commission-only salespeople would be deemed direct expenses, as would sales taxes that are collected and paid only upon the occurrence of revenue generation. Payroll taxes for employees who get paid regardless of sales are considered an operating expense along with their associated payroll.

Gains or losses on stocks also are "below the operating line," or nonoperating expense items, because the investments are not necessarily correlated with the company's performance. These gains or losses are often deemed to be one-time charges or benefits due to their nonrecurring nature. An example of what is generally deemed a one-time expense is a restructuring charge, which is a cost of making a large organizational change, such as a mass layoff along with the associated severance payments to the terminated workers as well as other costs like plant closings or office consolidation moving expenses.

Another nonoperating item is the net income or loss associated with discontinued operations. Once a company makes plans to sell or liquidate a portion of its business, the net result of the piece being sold is labeled "discontinued" and is included as a nonoperating item. This is done because the inclusion of these segments with continuing operations would mislead investors about the future consistency of operating income.

For what it is worth, some companies might consider advertising (or other items considered here to be operating costs) to be a direct expense.

The more important issue is not whether an expense is classified as direct or indirect but rather the timing of the recording and the amount the expense being recorded. A recent example of differing expense classifications is illustrated in the accounting statements of International Business Machines Corporation (IBM) and Hewlett-Packard Company (HP) in their provisions for restructuring costs within their service businesses. IBM considers restructuring costs to be operating expenses, while HP views them as nonoperating costs (below the line).

Despite IBM's absorption of such costs as operating expenses, IBM has a 15 percent operating margin on its services business. HP, even without the restructuring cost burden on operating expenses, has only a 13.8 percent operating margin on servicing. This is a significant difference and one that IBM touts as an example of its superior performance to the media as well as investors. The point here is that even large Fortune 500 companies have classification differences; prospective investors need to examine financial statements closely in order to determine apples-to-apples comparisons.

You can apply the principles of the income statement to any individual, business, or government agency, no matter how large or small. For example, each person brings in a certain amount of money for each year or other time frame (possibly coming from a job, rental income, or alimony) and must pay expenses (rent, electricity, grocery bills, clothes, gasoline, car maintenance, and insurance) during the same period. Whatever is left is that person's profit or loss. People who generate a personal annual profit are in a position to save or invest their profits for their future. Their subsequent interest or gains on those investments may also be considered income for future periods. On the other hand, those folks who aren't able to live within their means often need to increase debt each year to subsidize their cash flow deficiency. They may do so through mortgage refinancing to higher debt levels, increasing credit card balances, or allowing other bills to grow through nonpayment. These concepts apply equally well to individuals and companies.

To reiterate, it is very important to note that *not* everything you buy is an expense—at least not immediately. An expense is recorded only when the *value is lost*. When Jackie buys hammers, for example, she is only transferring one asset, cash, into another asset, inventory. It is only when the inventory becomes someone else's property through sale (or damage or theft, for that matter) that the value is lost and an expense is recorded. The purchase of real estate or equipment, similarly, does not cause an immediate loss of value and does not justify an immediate expense, as the value is not deemed to be lost at the time. The purchase of these assets simply shifts cash into different categories. The loss of the value of long-term assets is gradual and is taken into account in a different manner.

More about this later. Let's first look at the balance sheet components piece by piece.

2

ASSETS

Assets are simply things a company owns. A company might own cash, equipment, trademarks, real estate, IOUs from customers, pending tax refunds, inventory, or marketable securities. Assets are generally broken into two categories: short-term (or current) assets and long-term assets. Companies don't own people (their employees), but it might feel that way sometimes!

CURRENT ASSETS

Current assets are those things a company owns that are expected to be turned into (or used as) cash within one year from the date they're listed on the balance sheet. Examples of current, or short-term, assets include cash, short-term investments, IOUs from customers (accounts receivable), prepaid expenses, and inventory. The total of all current assets (less total current liabilities) determines a company's working capital (see "Working Capital and Liquidity" in Chapter 5). The monetization of current assets provides the cash necessary to meet some of the funding needs of the business for the following year, including current liabilities.

Cash and Short-Term Investments

Cash, quite simply, is the amount of money on hand (for example, in a safe or cash register), plus the balances in all checking and savings accounts. Deposited cash often generates a small amount of interest, which is a source of nonoperating income. Short-term investments include loans to the U.S. government in the form of Treasury bills (loans of less than one year, as opposed to Treasury notes or bonds, which aren't due for at least a year). Other short-term investments such as certificates of deposit (CDs) and funds deposited in money market accounts are also lumped into this category. Short-term investments are included with cash because they are considered to be very safe and are liquid enough to be readily converted into cash, should the need arise.

At the end of the day, cash is king. The goal of every business is to create value for its owners. Value is often viewed as a company's ability to generate cash. There was a time in the late 1990s and early 2000s when misguided markets looked to Internet-based businesses to show maximum "eyeballs," or Web site visits. Such perceptions came from the mindset that (paying for) eyeballs in the present (through massive advertising campaigns) would lead to cash flow in the future. In this regard, companies were valued at many times their annual revenue and profit (or, more often, losses). Reality soon set back in thereafter, though, as the Internet bubble burst and share values plummeted.

Accounts Receivable and Prepaid Expenses

When a company ships an order, it is customary in many businesses to extend to that customer payment terms. Fifteen, thirty, or even ninety days may be granted to pay the invoice that accompanies the goods or services provided. From the period when the sale is recorded (which is generally when the transaction is completed and the corresponding invoice is generated and sent to the customer), until the point at which the funds are received, the company is owed money in the form of an IOU from the customer. Customer IOUs, which are quite common in most businesses that don't require payment in full upfront, are called "accounts receivable." Having accounts receivable equaling one month of sales (about 30 days) might be a reasonable level in many types of businesses. Accounts receivable assets, to the extent that they are current (and not past due), are often used as collateral for short-term loans, as they are likely to provide a business with cash in a month or two from the date listed on their balance sheet.

Not all businesses extend payment terms to customers. Restaurants, for example, generally require you to pay for a meal before leaving the premises (of course, there are exceptions, like Norm's running tab at *Cheers*). For restaurants that accept credit cards, payment might be withheld for a day or two by the credit card companies. For this short time period, the business would own a credit card receivable asset until it is converted into cash. Other business types, such as a patio installation company, may actually require customers to front money prior to any work being performed. This customer deposit (sometimes called deferred revenue), as opposed to an account receivable, is actually a company's

17

short-term liability because work is required to earn the money that has already been received. (See "Current Liabilities" in Chapter 3.)

Prepaid expenses reflect cash that has already been paid for items that have yet to be delivered. For example, if a business were to pay $1,000 monthly rent for six months in advance, it would have an asset equal to $6,000 on its balance sheet. Provided that it made no additional payments, its prepaid rent current asset would decline to $5,000 one month later (as its prepaid asset would now cover only five months). The $1,000 of value "used up" in that first month would be expensed on the income statement, even though no cash was spent at the time the value was purged. At the beginning of the six-month period, there is value to this cashless asset. After the six months is up, no residual value remains. Other examples of prepaid expenses are deposits a business may have placed on inventory orders that have yet to be delivered or a down payment on an insurance policy when the premiums have not yet been earned.

One reason that insurance premiums are offered as pay-as-you-go to even poor credit businesses and individuals is that there is always a prepaid balance. Once the insured falls behind in the amount paid versus the amount earned, the policy is canceled. In short, the premium finance company takes little risk and may offer financing at reasonable rates as a result.

Prepaid expenses save a company from having to lay out cash for short-term expenses. All else being equal, a company with prepaid expenses will see cash balances rise faster than net income because some future expenses have already been funded.

Financially strong businesses generally don't need to utilize prepayments. They may do so, however, if a sufficient discount is offered to justify the advance payment. For example, if your company seeks to sell products to (and through) Wal-Mart, and Wal-Mart insists on taking

90 days to pay you, you'd still likely pursue the transaction. If your business was hurting for cash, you might ask (humbly) to be paid sooner in exchange for a lower price to the giant retailer. (See "Working Capital and Liquidity" in Chapter 5 for more information.)

Inventory

When you walk into a Wal-Mart, your local grocery store, or even a gas station, you'll see shelves of items previously purchased by the business and available for sale. These items for sale are called "inventory." Obviously, each business pays less for the inventory than it hopes to receive from customers in the future in order to generate a gross profit. Not all businesses require inventory, though. For example, a consultant may be paid for advice and does not need to carry goods to be sold. But many retail establishments, including restaurants, landscape nurseries, electronics stores, and lemonade stands, must use cash in advance to have items available for sale later. And inventory can be a costly proposition. In order to have a full selection, a business may have to stock items that don't sell quickly so that customers visit the establishment to fulfill many of their purchase requirements. Home Depot, Staples, Wal-Mart, and Macy's are all examples of companies that carry a wide variety of goods, even though some items are not sold frequently. So much of those companies' cash is tied up for extended periods without providing a quick return on the investment.

In the case of Jackie's Hardware Store, from Chapter 1, it stocks hammers, nails, paint, hoses, fertilizer, ladders, and many other products. Some items provide a high gross margin; others significantly lower. But in order to induce customers to make the trip, Jackie carries screws and bolts in every size so that customers will be confident that making the trip to Jackie's Hardware Store will be worthwhile. Maintaining inventory levels is a substantial use of her available cash resources. She may pay for items that sit on her shelves for years. At some point, these older items may be reduced in price in order to facilitate their disposition. These markdowns to get rid of older or obsolete inventory reduce her gross profit margin, but they may help her to raise needed cash at some point in the future.

Again, it is very important to note that the purchase of inventory is not considered an immediate expense. The expense is recorded when the value is lost. When a customer purchases a hammer and Jackie no longer owns it, she must recognize that her inventory base has been reduced. She then expenses her cost of that hammer while recording the price received for the hammer as a sale, or revenue. If an item were stolen or broken, and no longer salable, she would record the expense as value having been lost, but she would not recognize the corresponding revenue, as no purchase would have occurred. Whether a hammer is stolen, broken, or sold to a customer, the object loses its value upon any of these occurrences. When any of these situations, or "trigger events," occurs, the business is required to recognize the lost value, and the item is expensed at that point.

In Jackie's case, her short-term assets at the end of last year consisted of $100,000 of cash, $50,000 of accounts receivable, and $150,000 of inventory. Her total short-term assets therefore were $300,000:

Jackie's Short-Term (Current) Assets

Cash	$100,000
Receivables	50,000
Inventory	150,000
Total Current Assets	$300,000

NONCURRENT ASSETS

Noncurrent, or long-term, assets are those things a company owns that are not expected to be converted into or used as cash within one year. Noncurrent assets are generally utilized in the operation of a business. Examples include equipment, furniture and fixtures, real estate, patents, trademarks, and long-term investments.

Equipment

Types of equipment will vary from one business to the next. A construction company may have cranes, dump trucks, and bulldozers. A warehouse might utilize forklifts. A newspaper business requires large printing presses. Each of them probably has copiers, computers, and some furniture. In all of these cases, however, equipment is utilized to facilitate operations to make them more efficient. Laborers could dig a big hole with their hands, but doing so would take a long time, and the process would be cost-prohibitive. A backhoe can accomplish the same objective in a much shorter time frame at a drastically reduced cost. Twenty strong men might lift a large box onto a warehouse shelf but would risk personal injury and damage to the stored items. They are grateful for the forklift's help. Computers help organize deliveries, facilitate record keeping, prepare professional sales presentations, and access research and news via Internet portals. Cars and trucks are often deemed a form of equipment—imagine the loss of productivity a business would suffer without them! In general, equipment may be viewed as an efficiency-enhancing tool that provides operational benefits to a business for years. These long-term assets are critical components to keeping companies competitive. As you might imagine, different types of equipment have varying productive, or useful, life spans.

Real Estate and Related Improvements

Companies often own the land and buildings in which they do business and may own other real estate as an investment as well. These long-term assets generally hold their value for many years. Owning the occupied real estate eliminates the need to pay rent and avoids a landlord's lease renewal demands but subjects the company to pay real estate taxes as well as associated insurance costs.

The purchase of real estate is not deemed to be an immediate loss of value and is therefore not expensed at the time of acquisition—it is a transfer of one asset, cash, to another, the land and building. Similarly, the cash paid for improvements to the real estate, such as a new roof, an addition, a new electrical system, or aluminum siding are not immediate expenses. Real estate and improvements are listed on the balance sheet at their original cost. Much like the purchase of equipment, these cash outlays produce lasting benefits. For this reason, the loss of value of real estate and related improvements occurs gradually. Land, on the other hand, is never deemed to lose value (although you might disagree if your beach house sinks underwater through sand erosion).

Like accounts receivable and to a lesser degree, inventory, real estate has historically been an excellent security for a loan due to its long-term value. Because land and buildings have such an extended estimated useful life (39.0 years for commercial property, 27.5 years for residential real estate), the financing available for their purchase has a much longer payback period than shorter-term assets like accounts receivable (or even equipment). Assets related to real estate are expensed over many years. (See "Depreciation and Amortization" in Chapter 5 for more details on this process.)

Investments

Companies, like individuals, seek to utilize their resources in an efficient manner. If assets are available, management is evaluated on how well it is able to generate a return on the pool of resources it has to invest. Smart managers will constantly survey market opportunities and will consider seeking ownership of equity in other companies, debt obligations that provide a steady return, commodities that may be useful as a business hedge (like an airline committing to long-term fuel supply contracts), or currency hedging transactions (which may also be beneficial for businesses that derive sales from countries that utilize denominations other than their own). Such hedging transactions might "lock in" an exchange rate for the importation of goods from foreign jurisdictions or the sale of products to other countries for a period of time. While these investments might lose money, some businesses consider them to be analogous to insurance premiums in that they to smooth out otherwise volatile operating results. Companies that do not hedge future costs for commodities needed for production generally believe that the cost of doing so is excessive, that prices will decline over the short to medium term, or that they will be able to pass along higher future costs to their customers.

For example, Southwest Airlines has tended to hedge a greater portion of its jet fuel requirements than most other major domestic airlines. By locking in a predetermined price for future purchases, Southwest has been able to stabilize its operating results. When jet fuel prices soared in 2008, many carriers had trouble covering their fuel costs with revenue from air fares and package deliveries. This resulted in billions of dollars of industry losses and several prominent bankruptcies. Southwest, however, remained profitable and saved approximately $3.5 billion through fuel hedging from 1999 through 2008.

Such investments are also initially listed on a company's balance sheet at their initial cost. However, their balance sheet values tend to be more volatile than other assets, like real estate and equipment. The fluctuation in the carrying, or book value, of these assets is recorded as a nonoperating gain or loss on the income statement.

Intangible Assets

Intangible assets, quite simply, are things a company owns that you can't touch or feel. Intellectual property, such as patents, trademarks, and copyrights, are prime examples of intangible assets. The cost of acquiring or developing such items is recorded as a long-term asset on a company's balance sheet. These types of assets protect a business from others infringing on its efforts to create or buy something new, such as a brand, logo, book, or drug. In this fashion, companies have a greater motivation to spend time and money to develop such property knowing that a period of exclusivity accompanies these creations. It wouldn't be fair, for example, for a new company to start selling cereal called Fruit Loops with packaging identical to Kellogg's. Kellogg Company has spent millions on customer awareness of the brand—but wouldn't have done so without intellectual property protection.

A patent is a set of exclusive rights granted by a government to an inventor or his or her assignee for a limited period of time in exchange for a disclosure of an invention. In short, patents protect an inventor by restricting others from copying his or her invention (which may be a useful tool or process).

The procedure for granting patents and the extent of the exclusive rights varies widely among countries according to national laws and international agreements. Typically, however, a patent application must include one or more claims defining the invention which must be new, inventive, and useful or industrially applicable. In many countries, certain subject areas are excluded from patents, such as business methods and mental acts. The exclusive right granted to a patentee in most countries is the right to *prevent others* from making, using, selling, or distributing the patented invention without permission for a period of time.

There are three types of patents:

1. *Utility patents.* These may be granted to anyone who invents or discovers any new and useful process, machine, article of manufacture, or composition of matter, or any new and useful improvement thereof such as an artificial heart valve.
2. *Design patents.* These may be granted to anyone who invents a new, original, and ornamental design for an article of manufacture, such as the look of the original Macintosh computers.
3. *Plant patents.* Anyone who invents or discovers and asexually reproduces any distinct and new variety of plant, such as a new variety of an almond tree, may be granted a plant patent.

For example, patents are granted to pharmaceutical manufacturers for developments such as Pfizer's Viagra drug. After a time of exclusivity, generic drug makers are then permitted to use the same composition of matter under different brand names.

Trademarks

A trademark is a distinctive sign or indicator used by an individual, business organization, or other legal entity to identify that the products or services to consumers with which the trademark appears originate from a unique source, and to distinguish its products or services from those of other entities. In short, trademarks protect logos and/or brief phrases.

A trademark is designated by the following symbols:

™(for an *unregistered trademark*, that is, a mark used to promote or
    brand goods)
SM(for an *unregistered service mark*, that is, a mark used to promote
    or brand services)
®(for a *registered trademark*)

A trademark is a type of intellectual property; typically, a name,
word, phrase, logo, symbol, design, image, or a combination of these
elements used to indicate the source of the goods and to distinguish
them from the goods of others. A service mark is the same as a trademark except that it identifies and distinguishes the source of a service
rather than a product. The terms "trademark" and "mark" are com-
monly used to refer to both trademarks and service marks. Examples of
trademarks are the Nike swoosh and Apple Computer's Apple.

Trademark rights may be used to prevent others from using a confus-
ingly similar mark, but not to prevent others from making the same goods
or from selling the same goods or services under a clearly different mark.

Copyrights

A copyright is a form of protection provided to the creators of "original
works of authorship," including literary, dramatic, musical, artistic, and
certain other intellectual works, both published and unpublished. A copyright generally gives the owner of the intangible asset the exclusive right
to reproduce the copyrighted work, to prepare derivative works, to distribute copies or phonorecords of the copyrighted work, to perform the
copyrighted work publicly, or to display the copyrighted work publicly.

The copyright protects the form of expression rather than the subject matter of the writing. For example, a description of a machine could be copyrighted, but doing so would prevent others only from copying the description; it would not prevent others from writing a description of their own or from making and using the machine.

The copyrighting process has been internationally standardized, lasting between 50 to 100 years from the author's death, or for a shorter period of time for anonymous or corporate authorship.

Developed Technology

Another form of intangible asset is developed technology. Developed technology may also be recorded as an intangible asset, even if a patent or copyright is not yet issued, to protect the exclusivity of the project. To illustrate the appropriateness of this procedure, imagine that Johnson & Johnson (J&J) decides to develop a cancer drug. The money spent on research is not being lost. It may be capitalized, or added to, the intangible asset, which is the "Drug Under Development" (see "Expensing versus Capitalizing" in Chapter 5).

Years may pass with continued additions to this asset category through incremental funding until it reaches commercial acceptance and receives approval from the U.S. Food and Drug Administration. At that time, J&J would estimate the drug's future sales over many years and would expense this drug over the corresponding period along with the sales as they occur (see "Depreciation and Amortization" in Chapter 5). On the other hand, if the drug proves to be ineffective, unsafe, or both, the drug might be fully expensed, or written off, at that time (see "Write-downs and Write-offs" in Chapter 5), as the value would be deemed to have been completely lost.

Goodwill

Another type of intangible asset is goodwill. Goodwill is recorded when a business is purchased for a value in excess of its tangible assets. The difference between the purchase price and the tangible asset value is a long-term asset called "goodwill." For example, if a company has tangible assets of $1 million and is purchased for $3 million, the buyer would record the transaction as a use of cash of $3 million. Cash would be reduced by $3 million, and appropriate tangible asset categories, such as equipment, real estate, and accounts receivable, would increase by their respective proportions of the $1 million.

The difference of $2 million would reflect the difference between the amount paid and the otherwise allocated tangible assets as goodwill. To look at goodwill from another angle, a company's value is more clearly demonstrated in the amount of operating profit and income it is able to generate than the assets it carries on its balance sheet. If a business earns $1,000,000 each year but has tangible assets of only $500,000, the value of the enterprise clearly exceeds the company's tangible asset value. In this case, the managers of the business are doing very well managing the tools at their disposal. The company that earns $1 million annually might have a total value to a buyer of $10 million. But with only $500,000 of assets, the buyer would need to record the difference, or $9,500,000, as goodwill upon the acquisition of the company. Don't think that the buyer necessarily overpaid, though. As long as the income holds up, the purchase generates a 10 percent rate of return ($1 million of profit divided by the $10 million purchase price) even without using leverage to consummate the transaction or reaping potential synergies from the acquisition.

At the end of last year, Jackie's Hardware Store had long-term assets totaling $1.5 million. These consisted of $200,000 of equipment, $200,000 worth of furniture and fixtures, and $1,100,000 of real estate and related improvements:

Jackie's Long-Term Assets

Equipment	$ 200,000
Furniture and Fixtures	200,000
Real Estate and Improvements	1,100,000
	$1,500,000

It is important to note that a company's assets have both a market value and a book value. The market value is the amount the business would receive if the assets were sold today on an orderly basis. The book value is the accounting mechanism by which the entries are input onto the balance sheet. Market and book values are not always the same. (We'll explain why in Chapter 5.)

Just as a company has possessions of various types, it also is obligated to pay various creditors. It is important to understand both sides of the balance sheet, so let's now move on to a description of liabilities.

3

LIABILITIES

Liabilities are simply monies that a company owes. A business might owe money to the Internal Revenue Service in the form of taxes, to employees in the form of accrued payroll, to vendors in the form of accounts payable, or to banks for credit cards, mortgages, and other loans. You might have a car loan, mortgage, electric bill, or hospital invoice or owe taxes in much the same fashion as a company. Liabilities show how much cash will be needed (beyond weekly operating expenses) to pay obligations that come due within the next year (current liabilities) and beyond (long-term liabilities).

CURRENT LIABILITIES

Recall that current assets are expected to be used as or converted into cash within one year. Similarly, current liabilities are those obligations, which the company must pay within 12 months from the date of the balance sheet on which the current liabilities are shown. Examples of current liabilities are accounts payable, accrued expenses, customer deposits, and that portion of long-term debt's principal that is due within a year.

Accounts payable are IOUs effectively issued by a company when it receives goods or services from vendors. These short-term obligations may include an electric bill or an invoice for goods received that has not yet been paid. In Jackie's case, at any given time, Jackie's Hardware Store owes money for utility bills and to suppliers of such products as hoses, light bulbs, screwdrivers, tiles, and rakes. These suppliers generally expect to be paid within 30 days of Jackie's receipt of the products, which is accompanied by an invoice detailing the obligation.

Accrued Expenses

Accrued expenses are another form of current liabilities. These obligations generally grow, or accrue, over time without a corresponding invoice detailing the debt. For example, employees in a business might have the benefit of four paid weeks of vacation each year. If and when each employee leaves the company, he or she is entitled to be paid for unused vacation time. To accurately reflect that the company owes this money, an expense is recorded above cash payroll expenses each period in which the vacation time is not taken. Assuming that this benefit is not utilized, each calendar quarter one week of an employee's pay would be expensed as a recognized obligation, and the amount owed would be added to the accrued expenses category. When the person leaves the company, cash would need to be used to pay off the then-current balance of his or her accrued vacation time, and accrued expenses would decline accordingly.

Another example of an accrued expense would be payroll. If a balance sheet were to be dated at the end of the day on a particular Wednesday, and Jackie's employees receive paychecks every Friday, the balance sheet must reflect the liability for three days (Monday through Wednesday) of accrued payroll liability, even though she hasn't received an invoice reflecting such obligation.

While it may not seem immediately obvious, another type of current liability is customer deposits. Imagine that a carpenter agrees to install a new deck on your house. The agreed-upon price for the job is $12,000. In order for the carpenter to fund his or her upfront costs associated with the purchase of materials necessary to commence work, a deposit of one-third of the job's value, or $4,000, is required at the signing of the contract. The carpenter has now received $4,000 but has not yet delivered the agreed-upon product. At this moment, he or she has essentially borrowed the $4,000 advance from you, the homeowner.

Until the work is performed and the loan is essentially repaid through completion of the contracted work, the carpenter must recognize the $4,000 liability on his or her balance sheet as a customer deposit. If you, the homeowner, still haven't paid the carpenter the balance of $8,000, despite the project being properly finished, the carpenter's $4,000 for the customer deposit would become an $8,000 account receivable on his or her books. The loan *to* him or her would become a loan *from* him or her now that the work is complete.

Short-Term Portion of Long-Term Obligations

Long-term debt obligations, such as equipment loans or mortgages on real estate, generally require repayment over a period no longer than the estimated useful life of the asset, which is used as the collateral to secure repayment. Some long-term debt obligations have no underlying collateral, meaning that they are *un*secured but are payable over a multiyear period, such as credit cards. Some long-term debt obligations require a large lump-sum payment at a point in the future, called a "balloon payment."

Most long-term debt loans have a fixed monthly payment for a specified number of months. In these self-amortizing structures, the first payment is mostly interest (the cost of borrowing the money), and the last payment is mostly principal (the repayment of the loan). In this fashion, a business may pay off its obligation without the burden (and associated risk) of having a large single (balloon) payment to make. In order to calculate how much a monthly payment would be, the interest rate and duration of the loan must be determined. The resulting calculation results in an amortization table. The amortization table shows how much of each fixed payment represents interest and how much is allocated to principal. The longer the repayment period and the higher the interest rate, the greater the initial percentage of payments allocated to interest. An example of an amortization table for a $100,000, five-year loan, with monthly payments at 8 percent is shown in Table 3.1 on pages 36–37. As you can see, the current portion of this loan is $16,944, which represents the sum of the principal portion of the first 12 monthly payments.

Once an amortization table is established for an equipment loan, for example, a company may add up the principal portion due for each of the next 12 monthly payments following a balance sheet's date. The sum of these 12 varying (and increasing) principal portions of the equipment loan payments would be listed on the balance sheet as the current portion of long-term debt. In other words, even though the equipment loan might be a five-year obligation, the portion of principal that must be repaid in the next year is a short-term liability, and the remainder still is a long-term liability. The portion of each payment that is allocated to interest is expensed as incurred as the value is lost. Repayments of principal are simply the use of an asset (cash) to reduce the liability (the equipment loan).

In the case of Jackie's Hardware Store, from Chapter 1, at the end of last year, Jackie had short-term liabilities of $100,000, consisting of $50,000 of accounts payable and $50,000 of accrued expenses.

LONG-TERM LIABILITIES

Just like long-term assets, which are not expected to be converted into or used as cash within one year from their posting on a balance sheet, long-term liabilities are not required to be paid for at least one year. Examples of long-term liabilities include real estate mortgages, equipment loans, bonds, or bank debt. Of course, some or all of these obligations might be due in the upcoming 12 months, depending on their maturity dates and whether or not some of the principal might be required to be paid in the short run.

MORTGAGE LIABILITIES

Examples of debts that needn't be paid for at least a year include loans secured by real estate, or mortgage liabilities. Much like the loan you may have secured to help finance the purchase of a home, mortgage liabilities are used by companies to provide relatively inexpensive capital. The loan secured by real property (land or buildings) is often less expensive (i.e., at a lower interest rate) than unsecured loans because the collateral provided reduces the risk to the lender should a payment default occur.

Secured loans often have an amortization period (a time frame for loan repayment), which to some degree correlates to the estimated

Table 3.1 Sample Amortization Table for $100,000 Borrowed on February 1, 2010

Month	3	4	5	6	7	8	9	10	11	12	1	2
Year	2010	2010	2010	2010	2010	2010	2010	2010	2010	2010	2011	2011
Payment ($)	2,027.64	2,027.64	2,027.64	2,027.64	2,027.64	2,027.64	2,027.64	2,027.64	2,027.64	2,027.64	2,027.64	2,027.64
Principal Paid ($)	1,360.97	1,370.05	1,379.18	1,388.37	1,397.63	1,406.95	1,416.33	1,425.77	1,435.27	1,444.84	1,454.48	1,464.17
Interest Paid ($)	666.67	657.59	648.46	639.27	630.01	620.69	611.31	601.87	592.37	582.80	573.16	563.47
Total Interest ($)	666.67	1,324.26	1,972.72	2,611.99	3,241.99	3,862.69	4,474.00	5,075.87	5,668.23	6,251.03	6,824.20	7,387.66
Balance ($)	98,639.03	97,268.98	95,889.80	94,501.43	93,103.80	91,696.85	90,280.52	88,854.75	87,419.48	85,974.64	84,520.16	83,055.99

Month	3	4	5	6	7	8	9	10	11	12	1	2
Year	2011	2011	2011	2011	2011	2011	2011	2011	2011	2011	2012	2012
Payment ($)	2,027.64	2,027.64	2,027.64	2,027.64	2,027.64	2,027.64	2,027.64	2,027.64	2,027.64	2,027.64	2,027.64	2,027.64
Principal Paid ($)	1,473.93	1,483.76	1,493.65	1,503.61	1,513.63	1,523.72	1,533.88	1,544.11	1,554.40	1,564.76	1,575.20	1,585.70
Interest Paid ($)	553.71	543.88	533.99	524.03	514.01	503.92	493.76	483.53	473.24	462.88	452.44	441.94
Total Interest ($)	7,941.37	8,485.25	9,019.24	9,543.27	10,057.28	10,561.19	11,054.95	11,538.48	12,011.72	12,474.60	12,927.04	13,368.98
Balance ($)	81,582.06	80,098.30	78,604.65	77,101.04	75,587.41	74,063.68	72,529.80	70,985.69	69,431.29	67,866.53	66,291.33	64,705.64

Month	3	4	5	6	7	8	9	10	11	12	1	2
Year	2012	2012	2012	2012	2012	2012	2012	2012	2012	2012	2013	2013
Payment ($)	2,027.64	2,027.64	2,027.64	2,027.64	2,027.64	2,027.64	2,027.64	2,027.64	2,027.64	2,027.64	2,027.64	2,027.64
Principal Paid ($)	1,596.27	1,606.91	1,617.62	1,628.41	1,639.26	1,650.19	1,661.19	1,672.27	1,683.42	1,694.64	1,705.94	1,717.31

Interest Paid ($)	431.37	420.73	410.02	399.23	388.38	377.45	366.45	355.37	344.22	333.00	321.70	310.33
Total Interest ($)	13,800.35	14,221.08	14,631.10	15,030.33	15,418.71	15,796.15	16,162.60	16,517.97	16,862.20	17,195.20	17,516.90	17,827.23
Balance ($)	63,109.37	61,502.46	59,884.83	58,256.43	56,617.16	54,966.97	53,305.78	51,633.51	49,950.09	48,255.46	46,549.52	44,832.21

Month	3	4	5	6	7	8	9	10	11	12	1	2
Year	2013	2013	2013	2013	2013	2013	2013	2013	2013	2013	2014	2014
Payment ($)	2,027.64	2,027.64	2,027.64	2,027.64	2,027.64	2,027.64	2,027.64	2,027.64	2,027.64	2,027.64	2,027.64	2,027.64
Principal Paid ($)	1,728.76	1,740.28	1,751.88	1,763.56	1,775.32	1,787.16	1,799.07	1,811.06	1,823.14	1,835.29	1,847.53	1,859.85
Interest Paid ($)	298.88	287.36	275.75	264.08	252.32	240.48	228.57	216.57	204.50	192.35	180.11	167.79
Total Interest ($)	18,126.11	18,413.47	18,689.22	18,953.30	19,205.62	19,446.10	19,674.67	19,891.24	20,095.74	20,288.09	20,468.20	20,635.99
Balance ($)	43,103.45	41,363.17	39,611.28	37,847.72	36,072.40	34,285.24	32,486.17	30,675.11	28,851.97	27,016.67	25,169.15	23,309.30

Month	3	4	5	6	7	8	9	10	11	12	1	2
Year	2014	2014	2014	2014	2014	2014	2014	2014	2014	2014	2015	2015
Payment ($)	2,027.64	2,027.64	2,027.64	2,027.64	2,027.64	2,027.64	2,027.64	2,027.64	2,027.64	2,027.64	2,027.64	2,027.64
Principal Paid ($)	1,872.24	1,884.73	1,897.29	1,909.94	1,922.67	1,935.49	1,948.39	1,961.38	1,974.46	1,987.62	2,000.87	2,014.21
Interest Paid ($)	155.40	142.91	130.35	117.70	104.97	92.15	79.25	66.26	53.18	40.02	26.77	13.43
Total Interest ($)	20,791.39	20,934.30	21,064.65	21,182.35	21,287.32	21,379.47	21,458.71	21,524.97	21,578.15	21,618.17	21,644.94	21,658.37
Balance ($)	21,437.06	19,552.33	17,655.04	15,745.10	13,822.43	11,886.94	9,938.55	7,977.16	6,002.70	4,015.08	2,014.21	0.00

useful life of the corresponding asset. Obviously, a lender doesn't want to extend a 100-year loan on a computer, which might be useful for only five years or so. If the borrower were to default 10 years from the loan origination date, he or she would have no collateral of significant value while the vast majority of the principal would still remain outstanding. In other words, most of the loan would effectively be *un*secured.

Because real estate, which has a very long estimated useful life (39.0 years for commercial real estate, 27.5 years for residential income property, for accounting purposes) is used as the security for mortgage liabilities, the loan amortization period is quite long. A 30-year mortgage is fairly standard in the industry. With a reasonable down payment, the lender will never be "underwater" even with such a long repayment period. This is largely due to the "self-amortizing" nature of most mortgages. Self-amortizing, simply put, means that a fixed monthly payment is split between principal (or repayment of the loan) and interest (the cost of borrowing the funds). The longer the amortization period (and to a lesser degree, the higher the interest rate), the greater the portion of the first few payments that is allocated to interest expense. Once the borrower has made most of the payments (say, 28 years into a 30-year mortgage), the vast majority of each payment constitutes principal repayment. The interest piece declines over the life of the loan.

For example, let's look at a $100,000 mortgage that requires monthly payments over 30 years at a fixed interest rate of 7 percent. Each of the 360 monthly payments (excluding any escrow payments for such things as real estate taxes, association dues, or insurance) would be $665.30. The first payment would consist of $81.97 of principal and $583.33 of interest. The interest piece initially is quite high, because you are paying interest on almost the full $100,000. It takes about 20 years (actually 20 years and 1 month) of the 30 years before the proportion of principal exceeds that of interest, with $332.98 of the monthly payment being allocated to debt reduction and $332.32 assigned to interest expense. The last, or three hundred sixtieth, payment is almost entirely principal, because there is very little debt remaining on which to charge interest. Of that last payment, $661.44 pays off the remaining principal while $3.86 covers your last interest expense. As you can see, all payment amounts remain the same despite varying splits along the way. Paying a little extra principal at the beginning of such a loan dramatically shortens the payoff time.

Note and Bond Liabilities

Note and bond liabilities are another means by which (generally large) businesses are able to raise capital for acquisitions, investments, equipment, and/or for general working capital purposes. Bond investors are generally unsecured (no collateral protection) and subordinated (junior in right of repayment) to bank loans, which mostly require collateral to secure repayment if a business fails.

For these reasons, bond interest rates, the payments of which are often made semiannually, are higher. Depending on the size of the company, its profitability, and its operating history, the cost of the capital will vary. In some instances, in order to reduce the cash cost of maintaining long-term bond debt, bond liabilities will include some kind of "equity kicker." This piece of upside, or additional, value brought by an ownership slice, which comes from the direct or indirect inclusion of some common equity, is designed to compensate the investor to accept a lower ongoing cash interest rate.

Payments on bonds are very frequently interest-only in nature. The payments are consequently smaller, but the principal is often due in a single, large balloon payment at the bond's maturity date (which can range from a couple of years to more than 50 years). Because, most of the time, the payments are 100 percent interest and the maturity date is more than a year away, all of the principal is considered a long-term liability (until the year prior to maturity).

Unsecured bonds and notes are lower on the capital structure than secured obligations, like bank loans (which often require accounts receivable or inventory as collateral for short-term loans and real estate or equipment as collateral for long-term loans), and are generally "pari passu" (or equal in line for repayment) with other unsecured debt, like trade payables owed to vendors. Unsecured bonds are senior in right of repayment to the different forms of equity, though.

As mentioned, note and bond liabilities, like preferred stock (see the next section), are in the middle of a company's capital structure, behind secured lenders like banks and other finance companies and ahead of common equity. For this reason, both bond liabilities and preferred stock are considered "mezzanine capital." (Ever sit in the middle deck at a baseball game or a concert?)

The only long-term liability for Jackie's Hardware Store at the end of last year was the $900,000 mortgage on the building in which the store is located. Her mortgage requires interest-only payments for the first three years and so, all of this debt is considered long term since the loan was originated, or lent, less than two years ago.

Jackie's Short-term (Current) Liabilities

Accounts Payable	$ 50,000
Accrued Expenses	50,000
Total	$100,000

Now I'll describe in greater detail the last major component of the balance sheet: equity, or net worth.

40

CHAPTER

4

EQUITY

Equity is simply the difference between assets and liabilities. If one were to sell all of a company's assets for their book value and use the proceeds to pay off all of its liabilities, what would be left over for the owners? Equity is also called "net worth." It represents the value that the owners have in the business.

In the example of Jackie's Hardware Store, Jackie's assets at the end of last year totaled $1.8 million, and her liabilities were $1 million. The difference between the two is her net worth, or equity, of $800,000:

Jackie's Net Worth

Assets	$1,800,000
Liabilities	−1,000,000
Net Worth	$ 800,000

NET WORTH or EQUITY: the value the owners have in the company.

Equity is composed of two primary components: *preferred stock* and *common stock*.

PREFERRED STOCK

Preferred stock, as the name implies, is "senior" to common stock. Preferred stock has a priority claim over common stock in the event that a company fails and is forced to liquidate or is restructured. With characteristics that often look more debtlike than equitylike, preferred stock often has an interest component and a maturity date. Several varieties of preferred stock exist.

Types of Preferred Stock

Investors who seek to purchase preferred stock appreciate the relatively senior nature of their claim while benefiting from the potential upside associated with common equity. If things go badly, they are paid prior to common shareholders. On the other hand, should a business prosper, preferred shares' value often increases dramatically along with common equity, though usually to a lesser degree.

Convertible Preferred Stock

Preferred shares that are *convertible* into common shares allow the holder to maintain senior status until such time as the conversion into common shares takes place. Imagine that an investor provides a company with a $1 million cash infusion. In return, the firm issues to the investor preferred shares that carry a 10 percent cash interest rate payable quarterly. Five years from the initial investment, the entire principal, or liquidation preference, of $1 million is due in full. In addition, however, the investor maintains the right (but not the obligation) during this time to convert the $1 million principal amount into 100,000 shares of common stock. This transaction would, in effect, be using the investor's claim of $1 million to purchase common shares at $10 each. At the time the investment was made, the company's shares were trading at $8 each.

If the company remains stable and its stock price remains constant during the five-year time frame, the investor would likely collect the 10 percent interest and receive the full investment back after five years. Should fortunes improve, though, as the investor hopes and expects, the company's shares might increase in value to $15 each during the time the preferred stock is outstanding. The investor might then utilize its option to convert the $1 million preferred claim into 100,000 shares of common stock. This transaction would dilute the existing common shareholders, each of whom would now own a smaller percentage of the company. On the other hand, the business would be relieved of its obligation to pay the $100,000 annual interest expense to preferred shareholders and by removing a senior claim, leave more value, in aggregate, to the common stock.

The conversion price of $10 is below the common share's trading price of $15, which is dilutive to the common shares at the time of conversion. However, the investment was made at the time the common stock was trading at $8 per share. Had the funds instead come in the form of common stock at the outset, 125,000 shares would have been issued ($1,000,000 divided by $8 per share) instead of the 100,000 shares that ultimately were provided.

Let's assume that the investor chooses to convert all of his or her preferred stock into common shares exactly one year after making the investment. The common stock is trading at $15 per share at the time the decision is made. The investor provided $1 million a year ago. Now, he or she has received $100,000 in cash (the 10 percent cash interest received during the year) plus 100,000 shares of common stock, worth $1.5 million ($15 per common share times 100,000 shares). In short, the investor now owns $1.6 million worth of cash and securities for an investment a year ago of $1 million, a 60 percent rate of return!

Both sides "win" here. The investor got some downside protection if things had gone south for the company prior to conversion and got a "wait-and-see" option to switch to common shares to captured upside if and when the business realized success. The company issued fewer shares of stock in exchange for providing the investor with said protection and ultimately realized less dilution for the investment than if the cash had come in the form of pure common stock at the outset.

Of course, if the business had faired poorly, the company's common stock price would probably have declined. The investor wouldn't have chosen to convert his or her claim into common shares at $10 each, and the business may have defaulted on paying the preferred stocks' liquidation preference, or principal, when due (or even the interest along the way, depending on the severity of the failure). To illustrate, if the company's common stock price had declined to $5 per share and the investor chose to convert his or her shares at $10 each, the result would be owning 100,000 shares of common stock worth $5 per share, or

$500,000. The investor would lose half of the value of his or her investment and, therefore, would not choose to utilize the conversion option. Instead, the investor would seek to maintain the senior status the preferred shares provide.

Convertible preferred shares may take many forms. In some cases, the convertible preferred shares *must* be converted into common shares after a predetermined period of time (Mandatory Convertible Preferred). There are cases where the interest must be or may be "paid in kind," or PIK. Paid in kind means that additional convertible preferred shares would be issued monthly, quarterly, semiannually, or annually instead of cash interest. In the example above, the investor's $1,000,000 of convertible preferred shares, if not converted into common shares, would grow to $1,100,000 face amount after one year and $1,210,000 face amount, or liquidation preference, after two years (10 percent accretion annually). Interest might also be paid to the investor by the company in the form of common shares.

Another interesting concept is when convertible preferred shares are convertible into common stock at a variable price per common share. Often a discount to the then-current common share price, the variable conversion factor creates a very favorable situation for the convertible preferred shareholders (with a very risky scenario for common stockholders). This is a bit more complex, so follow carefully. For purposes of this example, we'll exclude the likely impact of an interest component, whether in cash or PIK form. The company above, with its common stock trading at $8 per share, has 1 million shares outstanding and therefore has an $8 million market capitalization. It raises $1 million in convertible preferred stock. After the five years, the entire accrued amount is due in full. At any time in the interim, though, the investor may choose to convert the $1 million liquidation preference into common shares *at a 25 percent discount to the market price of the common shares with a minimum number of shares implied by initial conversion ratio.* If the conversion is made immediately, the investor would receive 166,667 common shares at a price of $6 each, implying a value of $1,333,333.

Sound too good to be true for the investor? The market for the common shares in this case is probably fairly illiquid, and the block of shares that would be received is not likely to fetch that price if shares all were attempted to be sold immediately. In the event that the common share price were to rise (which rarely happens with convertible preferred stock with a variable conversion price into common at a discount to market), the investor would fare even better. If the common share price rose to $10 per share, the investor would still get 166,667 shares (the minimum), which would be worth $1,666,667. In this case, the investor would own 14.3 percent of the company after conversion (166,667 shares issued divided by 1,166,667, the initial 1,000,000 shares plus the newly issued 166,667 shares).

The much more frequent scenario, however, is that the common stock price declines, even if the business prospects brighten somewhat. Let's look at the situation where the common share price declines to $4 each. The investor might convert his or her $1 million liquidation preference into shares at $3 each ($4 less the 25 percent discount). The investor in this case would receive 333,333 common shares for his or her claim, equating to 25 percent common equity ownership. A more dramatic example would be if the common stock price declined to $1 each. The conversion price would then decline to 75 cents each, resulting in 1,333,333 common shares necessary to satisfy the liquidation preference ($1,000,000 claim divided by $0.75). The vastly greater number of shares issued would now provide the investor with 57 percent of the company's common equity ownership [1,333,333 divided by 2,333,333 (the initial 1,000,000 shares plus the newly issued 1,333,333 shares)].

It is only after the conversion into common stock that the investor's interests are aligned with that of the other common shareholders' interests. Until that point, their motivations are in stark contrast.

It is not uncommon for this type of investor to try to manipulate the common share price downward in order to increase his or her ultimate ownership of the company. Such a pursuit may be accomplished through the aggressive sale of common shares by the investor through short selling. Short selling, or borrowing and then selling common stock without actual ownership, tends to lock in profit for the investor while increasing the investor's underlying company ownership. The borrowed shares that are sold may be returned via the common shares that are attained through conversion of the preferred at lower levels. This is why the variable conversion price convertible preferred stock that converts at a discount to then-current market is usually utilized (or accepted) by smaller public companies that are more needy (or desperate) for the cash.

COMMON STOCK

Ownership of *common stock* (in its various forms) represents possession of a piece of a company. Different business types have varying names for the certificates that identify their owners.

Types of Common Stock

Companies may be formed in different ways. The type of company that is formed will dictate the type of equity interests that are issued to the owners. Examples of business formation types are sole proprietorships, limited partnerships, limited liability companies, S corporations, and C corporations. These legal structures are important, especially for tax purposes. They are broadly broken into two categories: taxable entities and pass-throughs.

S corporations, limited liability companies, and partnerships generally do not pay income tax. Each owner is assessed his or her share of the annual profits from the business. Each company is required to file annual tax returns with the Internal Revenue Service (IRS), though. Such returns inform the IRS how much taxable income should be allocated to each owner. The owners receive a K–1 form, similar to an employee's W–2, to file along with their personal returns, which details the respective allocated profit or loss for the year.

C Corporations

C corporations, in particular, are subject to income tax on their annual taxable income. In addition, the owners or stockholders of a C corporation pay a second tax on any cash dividends that the company distributes to them each year. In short, shareholders of C corporations are subject to double taxation. There may be more than one class of common stock issued by C corporations. For example, Hershey's has two classes of common shares: one for insiders with super voting powers and one for everyone else.

While there is no requirement for C corporations to pay cash dividends to shareholders, the average large public C corporation has historically paid its owners approximately 30 percent of its after-tax net income.

C corporations provide their shareholders with significant protections from liabilities within the company that go unpaid. In other words C corporation creditors may look only to the assets of the business and may not, in almost all cases, "pierce the corporate veil" (see "Sole

Proprietorships" below) to seek any deficiency from the business owners. Most major companies—and many smaller ones—are treated as C corporations for federal income tax purposes. A corporation must file under Subchapter C of the tax code (and be deemed a C corporation) if it fails to meet even one requirement to qualify as an S corporation.

S Corporations

In general, *S corporations* do not pay any income taxes. Instead, the corporation's income or losses are divided among and passed through to its shareholders. The shareholders must then report the income or loss on their own individual income tax returns.

Unlike C corporations, S corporations are permitted only one class of stock. The maximum number of owners of an S corporation is 100, and each must be a U.S. resident for tax purposes. S corporation owners maintain significant liability protections, as do C corporation shareholders.

Limited Liability Companies

Limited liability companies (*LLCs*) have become the most popular choice for the creation of small to medium-sized businesses. Often described as the combination of a partnership and a corporation, the LLC combines a corporation's liability protection with a partnership's tax flexibility.

Like a sole proprietorship or partnership, an LLC enjoys pass-through taxation. This means that owners (also known as "members") report their share of profits or losses in the company on their individual tax returns. The Internal Revenue Service does not assess taxes on the company itself; thus, the double taxation that C corporations experience is avoided. LLC members can also elect for the IRS to tax their LLC as a C corporation or S corporation. Ownership interests in a limited liability company are called "membership interests."

LLC members benefit from limited personal liability for business debts and obligations. Members are not required to be U.S. citizens or permanent residents, and record keeping is relatively simple.

Partnerships

According to the Internal Revenue Service, a *partnership* is "the relationship existing between two or more persons who join to carry on a trade or business. Each person contributes money, property, labor or skill, and expects to share in the profits and losses of the business." The essential characteristics of this business form, then, are the collaboration of two or more owners, the conduct of business for profit (a nonprofit cannot be designated as a partnership), and the sharing of profits, losses, and assets by the joint owners. A partnership is not a corporate or separate entity; rather, it is viewed as an extension of its owners for legal and tax purposes, although a partnership may own property as a legal entity. There are two partnership types: general partnerships and limited partnerships.

In *general partnerships*, all of the partners are equally responsible for the business's debts and liabilities. In addition, all partners are allowed to be involved in the management of the company. In fact, in the absence of a statement to the contrary in the partnership agreement, each partner has equal rights to control and manage the business. Therefore, unanimous consent of the partners is required for all major actions undertaken. Be advised, though, that any obligation made by one partner is legally binding on all partners, whether or not they have been informed.

In a *limited partnership*, one or more partners are general partners, and one or more are limited partners. The general partners are personally liable for the business debts and judgments against the business; they can also be directly involved in the management. Limited partners are essentially investors (silent partners, so to speak) who do not participate in the company's management and who are also not liable beyond their investment in the business. State laws determine how involved limited partners can be in the day-to-day business of the firm without jeopardizing their limited liability.

General partners of either partnership type have no liability protection from creditors of the business. Not a good idea!

Sole Proprietorships

An individual may form a *sole proprietorship*, which is really just acting as an individual while using a company name. Sole proprietorships do not offer the individual protection from business liabilities, called a "corporate veil." A business with liabilities that can't be honored, sometimes resulting from litigation claims, may file for bankruptcy. In most cases, such a bankruptcy will limit any recovery for the creditors to the assets within the company. The sole proprietor does not have such protection, as the claims are against himself or herself personally.

Sole proprietorships are easy to establish and maintain, though. You don't have to file a separate business tax return or spend much to get started. Sole proprietorships may have employees as well. But with the danger associated with unlimited liability for business debts (and potential litigation claims), forming an LLC makes better sense.

Warrants

Warrants aren't really a form of company ownership. They are a *long-term option* to purchase common stock for a predetermined price for a specified time. For example, a company whose common shares trade at $10 each might sell an investor warrants to buy one million shares at $15 each for a period of five years for $2 million. The investor has effectively bought an option (not an obligation) to buy stock at $15 per share, a 50 percent premium to today's market price, for $2 per warrant. This investor is betting that the share price will rise to more than $17 per share over the next five years (to justify paying $2 to buy the shares at $15 each). Only if the price increases by more than this 70 percent figure will the warrants provide a positive return on his or her investment. In fact, if the stock price doesn't increase to at least $15 during this time, his or her outlay will become worthless. Because the "strike price" of $15 per share is greater than the current trading price, the option has no current intrinsic value. Consequently, it is deemed to be "out of the money" and has only option value (via the potential price increase within the remaining time before expiration). As time progresses, if the stock price does not increase, the option value will decline to zero as expiration approaches.

Warrants are very speculative, especially if the strike price (the predetermined cost per share) exceeds the current market price, and are consequently out of the money. If, during the five-year option period, the market price of the stock does not increase by 50 percent, the entire investment would be written off by the investor, but the funds received would be kept by the company. On the other hand, if the company's common share price were to increase by 20 percent annually for the five years, the stock would be worth about $25 per share ($10 would become $12 after one year, $14.40 after two years, $17.28 after three years, $20.74 after four years, and $24.88 after five years). The warrants would then have an intrinsic value of about $10 each (as the investor would be allowed to buy the stock for $10 under market).

Should this scenario materialize, an investor in the company's common stock would see a 150 percent return over this period ($25 per share less the $10 initial cost, or a roughly $15 profit on the $10 investment per share). The investor who chose to purchase the warrants, though, would see a much higher return (of 400 percent!) for the vastly heightened risk ($10 value per warrant less $2 initial cost, or an $8 profit on the $2 investment per warrant). If the common share price increased to only $14 per share during this time, though, the common stock buyer would have received a 40 percent return while, the warrant buyer would have lost his or her entire investment.

Sometimes, warrants are the form of equity participation that is provided to mezzanine capital investors in order to induce a prospective investor to produce the necessary cash and/or to reduce the cash interest rate associated with the bonds, notes, or preferred stock offerings.

The funds received by a company for the purchase of warrants is added to paid-in capital. The subsequent money from the warrant's exercise, if ever received, is also included in paid-in capital. To the extent, however, that the warrants are exercised at a price below the then current market price per share (which would likely be the only time an investor would choose to take advantage of the choice), the difference would be recorded as a nonoperating expense on the company's income statement. That would be done because more equity value would be issued than the amount of cash received in the transaction.

Paid-In Capital and Dividends

The book value of common stock consists of two components: paid-in capital and retained earnings.

Paid-in capital is the cash invested by a company's owners to help fund the business. This is not money that is payable at any specific time. It is not a loan. Paid-in capital is generally viewed as a long-term investment that does not burden the company with a repayment schedule. To the extent that a business prospers, some of the paid-in capital is at times distributed to the owners in the form of dividends. Quite simply, paid-in capital is money that shareholders provide to a business; dividends are payments returned from the company to its owners.

Note that business valuations vary. One owner may have provided $100,000 in paid-in capital at an early stage in the company's existence. At that time, since the firm had yet to generate any revenue and its future was uncertain, the owner may have received 33.3 percent of the ownership of the business, since the "pre–new money" valuation of the company was then deemed to be $200,000. (New money of $100,000 added to the existing $200,000 of company value yields $300,000 of value associated with the company, once the cash is received; $100,000 divided by $300,000 is 33.3 percent: one-third.) A second owner may have also provided $100,000 in paid-in capital a few years later.

But because the business has since started to thrive, now has a customer base, and is profitable, the agreed-upon valuation has dramatically increased. The pre–new money valuation for the second owner is determined to be $900,000. With the new $100,000 infusion, the total post–new money worth is calculated to be $1,000,000. The ownership percentage issued to the second owner would therefore be 10 percent, determined by dividing the new $100,000 by the total post–new money value of $1,000,000. The differing valuations for the two owners who invested the same amount of money are significant. While they each provided $100,000 of paid-in capital, the first owner owns 33.3 percent of the company (diluted down to about 30 percent from the new investment); the second, 10.0 percent.

The company now is prospering and generates extra cash beyond its operating needs. It decides to return some of the spare monies to its owners in the form of dividends. Assuming that the amount to be paid to owners is $75,000 annually, the first owner-investor will get 30 percent of this amount, or $22,500. The second owner-investor will receive $7,500.

In other words, the proportion of paid-in capital invested does not necessarily determine the ownership percentage or the allocation percentages for dividends—or company sale proceeds, for that matter.

Dividend yield is simply the amount of annual cash received by a shareholder by owning a single share of stock, divided by the share price. If a business pays its owners 50 cents per share each year and the share price is $10, the dividend yield is 5 percent. A higher payout generally is favored by investors. As a result, if dividends go up, the stock price often does also, keeping the dividend yield fairly constant. An unusually high dividend yield is often a signal that the company's ability and/or desire to maintain the same annual dividend level may be in peril.

Retained Earnings

A company's common equity benefits from two sources of funds. The first, *paid-in capital*, is infused by owners into the company outside of the business operations. The other, *retained earnings*, is the sum of all net income held from the company's inception. In short, these are profits that are kept in the company. If a firm loses money over an income statement's time frame, retained earnings on the balance sheet will decline by the amount of the losses. Similarly, paid-in capital on the balance sheet decreases by the amount of any dividends paid to owners over the same span.

MINORITY INTEREST

If a business owns more than 50 percent but less than 100 percent of another company, the balance sheet and income statement of the majority-owned business (partial subsidiary) are consolidated, or added, into the financial statements of the owner (partial parent) as though the partial subsidiary is wholly owned. Cash is added to cash, inventory is added to inventory, and so forth. On the income statement, revenue is added to revenue, direct costs to direct costs, and so on. An adjustment is necessary, however, to account for the portion of the company that is not owned. This adjustment is *minority interest*. If the majority-owed company has $1 million in shareholders' equity and the parent business owns 90 percent of the shares, the parent business does *not* own the other 10 percent. So an entry is made on the parent company's balance sheet in between liabilities and equity labeled "Minority Interest." In this case, the minority interest would be a $100,000 entry, calculated on the amount of the equity of the majority-owned subsidiary that is not owned by the parent: 10 percent of $1 million.

On the income statement, the nonowned portion of the majority-owned subsidiary also must be adjusted. After adding the full value (consolidating) of the parent and majority-owned subsidiary together, 10 percent of the net income from the mostly owned company needs to be backed out. For example, if the consolidation added $500,000 of annual profit to the parent (which still owns 90 percent), $50,000 would be expensed as a minority interest, nonoperating expense. If the consolidation resulted in a loss of $500,000 to the same parent, the stripping out of the 10 percent that is not owned would result in a $50,000 gain in the nonoperating results on the income statement.

Ownership of less than 50 percent of another company would not require consolidation of the two companies' financial statements. A single entry on the Long-Term Assets portion of the parent company's balance sheet would reflect the amount of the initial investment made in the unconsolidated subsidiary. Each year, this figure would increase or decrease on the balance sheet based on the portion of the partly owed subsidiary's income that is attributable to the parent's ownership percentage. A similar entry would be made in the nonoperating result portion of the parent's income statement called "profit or loss in unconsolidated subsidiaries."

Just like the income statement, a balance sheet may be utilized by an individual, business, or government agency of any size. Each person owns some assets (possibly a house, car, television, stocks, cash, or furniture). Adding them up and subtracting one's obligations at the same time (mortgage, credit cards, utility bills, etc.) yields one's personal net worth, or equity.

Now that we've described the balance sheet and income statement components, we'll now apply this knowledge to various accounting concepts. They should be much easier to digest with the tools provided so far.

5

BASIC ACCOUNTING PRINCIPLES AND METHODS

BASIC ACCOUNTING PRINCIPLES

There are two primary types of accounting that companies use: cash-based accounting and accrual-based accounting. Both are ethical and common. Each has its advantages for businesses, depending on their motivations and governing regulations.

CASH ACCOUNTING

Cash-based accounting is the simplest form of accounting. This is simply the process of recording revenue when the money is received from customers. On the other hand, expenses are recorded when checks are written to pay invoices. A company may essentially create financial statements from old bank statements with this method.

The problem with cash-based accounting is its accuracy. If a company, for example, receives many bills and has failed to pay them, no recognition of these obligations is reflected in the company's financial statements. The balance sheet shows no liability, and the income statement shows no expense.

Similarly, consider a company that has shipped many products and has already paid the bills associated with the fulfillment of said orders. If it hasn't yet gotten paid from customers yet, there is no recognition of the monies due. The company would look unprofitable on the income statement, and its equity would look low on its balance sheet, as there would be no corresponding accounts receivable assets.

Cash-based accounting is often preferred by small businesses. These firms are motivated by a desire to minimize, or defer, tax obligations. Such motivations might cause a company's officers to delay depositing checks received late in the year until early the following year. They might also pay bills in December that are actually attributable to expenses the following year, like insurance premiums, rent, or future advertising.

Neither the publisher nor I condone or endorse these practices. Nevertheless, it is important to understand how and why cash-based accounting is often utilized instead of accrual-based accounting.

Imagine a restaurant business that is suffering. The restaurant gets all of its revenue in immediate cash or relatively quick credit card payments. Bills from suppliers that provide napkins, dishes, and various food items as well as utility bills, rent, and insurance are not getting paid. These invoices are piling up, but the business lacks the cash to make the requisite payments. In cash-based accounting, these expenses don't show up. Revenue is recorded when cash is received and looks reasonably healthy. The restaurant may even look profitable due to the fact that expenses are not being recorded because they are not being paid. The reality is that the business is failing, but cash-based accounting makes the restaurant look inaccurately profitable.

On the other hand, a sneaker manufacturing company is doing very well. Current receipts are able to pay in full all outstanding bills, including those invoices associated with the fulfillment of a very large sneaker order. The order's materials, assembly costs, labor, payroll taxes, and shipping have all been paid. The only remaining item is the receipt of a check from the retailer that placed the order. The sneaker company may look even slightly unprofitable. The truth, however, is that, since all of the order fulfillment expenses have been paid, the pending future revenue will look like pure profit. Because the recognition of revenue occurs upon the receipt of funds, the income statement is skewed to look substantially less profitable than reality should dictate.

ACCRUAL-BASED ACCOUNTING

Accrual-based accounting provides a more accurate view of a company's financial picture than does cash-based accounting. Regardless of receiving or spending cash, companies that use accrual-based accounting record revenue when products or services are delivered or performed and customers are invoiced; expenses are recorded when bills are received. For this reason, accrual-based accounting is much more accurate. This book is based on the accrual method of accounting for this reason.

Assuming that bills ultimately get paid and receivables ultimately get collected, the primary difference between the two primary types of accounting is timing. Timing, however, is critically important when items get recorded on financial statements. We have discussed the fact that the income statement evaluates a company's revenue and expenses over a specific period of time and that a balance sheet shows a company's assets and liabilities at a specific point in time. To the extent that revenue, expenses, assets, or liabilities are recorded in time frames that don't reflect their actual activity, results may be substantially misleading.

Public companies are those in which you may purchase shares on an exchange. The acquisition of shares is actually the process of buying a piece of ownership in the business. Private companies, like the local Laundromat or Jackie's Hardware Store, do not have an easily available means of acquiring an ownership stake. Of course, if you approached Jackie with a pile of cash, she'd probably offer you a piece of her business, but the transaction would require documentation including a negotiated purchase and sale agreement.

Examples of public companies are International Business Machines (IBM), Microsoft, General Electric, and Delta Air Lines. These large, public companies are required to comply with *GAAP*, or Generally Accepted Accounting Principles, in recording and summarizing transactions. GAAP are based on the accrual method of accounting. These companies have a specific motivation: to maximize shareholder value. This process often involves trying to increase reported earnings per share so that the public share price is increased. Sometimes, the pressure from Wall Street to meet or exceed analyst's earnings expectations (and/or management bonus targets) is so great that public companies seek to accelerate revenues and slow down expenses, even though this process may be inefficient, tax-wise. Pushing for sales to be recorded in a company's fiscal quarter or year may tempt management into pursuing potentially unscrupulous practices in order to meet short-term earnings and stock price targets.

VALUING INVENTORY

As previously discussed, inventory is not expensed until the *value is lost*. In other words, when a customer buys an item and it is no longer owned by the business, the value is lost from the company's perspective and it is expensed at that time. Also, if an item is broken and not salable or if inventory is stolen, these would also be instances when an expense would occur.

Imagine, however, that Jackie had purchased 1,000 identical hammers. Five hundred (500) of the hammers cost her $4 each, and the other 500 had a unit price of $6. All are kept in her storeroom. If she sells a hammer for $10, would her direct cost, her cost of goods sold, be $4 with a resulting $6 gross profit, or would her direct cost be $6 and her gross profit $4? Let's consider our options.

FIFO VERSUS LIFO

FIFO is an acronym that stands for "first in, first out." First in, first out means that the first hammer Jackie purchased is the first to get expensed as the hammers are sold. If she bought the $4 hammers first, these would be the ones to be "sold" before any $6 hammers would get expensed.

LIFO stands for "last in, first out." The LIFO method of inventory selection for expensing purposes dictates that the most recent hammer Jackie purchased would be the first to be picked when a hammer is sold. In this case, since Jackie bought the $6 hammers most recently, they would be the ones to be expensed first.

In reality, it may not be possible to identify which inventory batch a hammer came from (there is just a box of 1,000 identical hammers in her warehouse), but for accounting purposes, she gets to effectively choose her gross profit sequence. The inventory expensing formula is therefore important to understand. In the notes to financial statements in a public company's annual report, the method utilized by a business is often clearly described. By evaluating whether a company's raw material or wholesale prices are going up or down and comparing that trend with its method for accounting for inventory expensing, a shrewd investor may be able to forecast gross margin trends for the business going forward. For example, an organization that chooses to utilize FIFO in a declining wholesale price environment is likely to see gross margin increase as the earlier purchases are worked off the balance sheet.

As a small business, Jackie's Hardware Store has flexibility regarding which method to apply. Jackie would likely utilize FIFO or LIFO, depending on whether her inventory costs are likely to rise or fall, so that she might defer profitability. She would choose FIFO if her inventory unit costs were in decline, as she'd be expensing the higher-priced goods first. On the other hand, LIFO would make more sense for her if her inventory pricing were rising (which it is, since her hammer unit cost has gone up from $4 to $6 each); she would then be expensing the higher-cost items first, delaying profits and, therefore, taxes. With LIFO, Jackie would lower her gross profit on the first 500 hammers to $4, which would lower her gross margin to 40 percent on the first 500 hammers sold. A large public company might take the opposite approach in an effort to maximize short-term profits to satisfy the Wall Street analysts by achieving or exceeding targeted quarterly earnings per share.

There is a third inventory valuation method as well, which is a hybrid between the last in, first out and first in, first out processes. The *average cost basis*, which combines all like items held in a company's inventory account on its balance sheet, simply takes a weighted average of the cost of the goods that are sold. Regarding

Jackie's hammers held in inventory, she would simply add the cost of the 500 six-dollar hammers ($3,000) to the cost of the 500 four-dollar hammers ($2,000); then she would divide the total cost of $5,000 by the 1,000 hammers in total to derive a unit cost per hammer of $5. This process reduces volatility with changing wholesale costs, as new purchases are continually averaged in with existing inventory on hand. For this reason, gross margin changes evolve more slowly with the hybrid method.

In some situations inventory values decline, sometimes precipitously, regardless of original cost.

WORKING CAPITAL AND LIQUIDITY

How much short-term cash is available to a business? One must factor in the need to pay current liabilities within a year (often quicker with accounts payable, for example). Then one would add cash and the expected monetization of current assets (such as the sale of inventory and receiving payments on accounts receivable) to derive a working capital figure. *Working capital*—simply current assets minus current liabilities—describes a company's liquidity position. *Liquidity* reveals a business' ability to respond to short-term problems and opportunities.

If Jackie were offered the opportunity to purchase inventory at a bulk discount from a competitor that was going out of business, her liquidity would likely determine her ability to consummate the purchase and take advantage of the situation. Banks that lend to small businesse very often look to current assets as collateral to secure loans and lines of credit. A typical lending ratio might be 80 percent of qualified accounts receivable plus 50 percent of inventory. This sum would dictate the amount of money the business would have available to draw upon for short-term needs in the form of a line of credit (like a revolving credit card). Such a lending facility allows companies to receive cash quickly to respond to ongoing business needs even though the receivables haven't been collected and the inventory has yet to be sold.

Unforeseen problems often arise as well. For example, a customer of Jackie's might have hurt himself with a nail gun he purchased at Jackie's Hardware Store. While she's sorry the accident occurred, Jackie would contend that the injury is not her fault. Regardless, a lawsuit might ensue. The cost of defending her business from the litigation can be substantial. Not only is she distracted with the effort necessary to appear in court and to attend depositions associated with the matter, but she is likely to hire attorneys to protect her interests. At several hundred dollars per hour, Jackie is forced to incur thousands of dollars of legal bills and expenses. She might even pay the plaintiff $5,000 not because she feels responsible, but because she calculates that ongoing legal bills and distractions are projected to be far more expensive. Her initial business plan did not foresee such costs. Having a cushion of liquidity would help her weather the storm until she is able to focus on her primary business activities again.

Imagine that a small sweater manufacturer receives a large order from Macy's Department Store, say for $1 million. The owner of the business is ecstatic! She then orders much more wool and thread, hires more people, pays for overtime, and purchases additional sewing machines and equipment. After several weeks of substantial additional cash outlays, the business completes the production process and pays to ship the order to Macy's warehouse, along with an invoice reflecting the $1 million bill for the sweaters. The sweater company then records an accounts receivable on its balance sheet. Macy's then may take 30, 60, or even 90 days to pay the manufacturer for the goods.

In the meantime, a huge amount of money has already been spent by the small business. The supplier of the wool and thread is screaming for its money. The equipment supplier is threatening to sue to take the machines back. But the sweater manufacturer does not have the cash to meet these obligations while it awaits payment from Macy's; its owner is losing sleep over the stress. These types of problems are fairly common with small companies that extend payment terms to their customers. On paper, the company is more profitable than ever, but it has less cash than ever due to its customer withholding payment. This is an example as to why profitability and liquidity are far from the same thing. How might this business meet the cash flow timing challenge?

One possible solution might be to offer Macy's a 2 or 3 percent discount to pay the invoice quickly, perhaps within 10 days. Yes, the $20,000 or $30,000 quick pay discount is painful, but it may allow the company to take advantage of another order being offered from Nordstrom. Without the cash infusion, this new opportunity would be lost.

Another avenue the sweater manufacturer might consider is receivables factoring. This is the process of selling or borrowing against the IOU from Macy's. The receivables factor, which could be a commercial bank or a specialty finance company, might pay the business $920,000 immediately upon the issuance of the bona fide invoice. When the $1 million is paid, the receivables factor would keep all of it. Again, the $80,000 "fee" is expensive, but the manufacturing company's viability might be preserved and subsequent business opportunities would remain available.

One additional method of managing the sweater company's cash flow would be to select vendors that are willing to wait along with the business for payment. Just as the sweater company is hungry for Macy's business, certain wool suppliers will seek additional business even if it means potentially delayed payment. In this fashion, the sweater manufacturer may better align its cash outlays and receipts.

MARKET VALUE VERSUS BOOK VALUE OF ASSETS

As mentioned earlier, assets are initially listed on a company's balance sheet at their cost. But in some situations the true market value of those assets may differ from their book value, sometimes greatly. For example, when you buy a new car and drive it for a month, it is generally worth considerably less than the price paid for it just a few weeks earlier. Conversely, a house that is purchased might increase in value over time. In both of these cases, the assets remain listed at their original cost on the balance sheet while the underlying market value may fluctuate. The *gradual* loss of value of long-term, or fixed, assets needs to be reflected annually on the income statement. Similarly, the balance sheet must show the declining worth of these assets.

DEPRECIATION AND AMORTIZATION

As mentioned earlier, the purchase of a long-term asset such as equipment or real estate is not considered an immediate expense, as the *value has not been lost* at the time of purchase. A business investing in a piece of equipment, for example, is simply transferring one asset, cash, into another asset, equipment. The value of said equipment does decline over time, however, as it gets older and becomes less useful.

When a long-term asset is purchased, a company must determine its *estimated useful life*. The estimated useful life is important to determine the period over which the asset's value is reduced to zero (or scrap value). Once this period of time is established, the business will record an annual noncash expense equal to the expected value loss during that year. This expense is called *"depreciation"* for tangible assets. The gradual loss of value for intangible assets like patents, trademarks, and copyrights is deemed *amortization*. Goodwill may no longer be simply amortized due to an accounting rule change.

For simplicity's sake, we did not discuss depreciation's effects on Jackie's Hardware Store when we summarized her financial statements earlier. But we'll now see how she feels the impact. Jackie, in an effort to facilitate the organization of inventory in her warehouse, decides to purchase a forklift for $70,000. She sits down with her accountant and decides that the forklift has an estimated useful life of seven years. So she chooses an accounting method called the "straight-line" depreciation formula. Straight line, as the name suggests, expenses an even amount of the asset's purchase each year over its estimated useful life. In this case, she expenses one-seventh of the cost of the forklift per year for each of the seven years of its estimated useful life, resulting in a $10,000 per year annual noncash direct expense for the forklift's gradual loss of value. This expense has the effect of reducing earnings for each year that the forklift is being expensed. It also reduces the book, or carrying, value of the asset by $10,000 each year. After one year from the purchase of the forklift, Jackie will have expensed one-seventh of its value, or $10,000, on the income statement. She'd then have a forklift in the Long-Term Asset section of her balance sheet with a reduced value of $60,000. After two years, she'd carry the asset at $50,000, and so on. Seven years later, Jackie will have expensed the entire cost of the forklift and will carry the asset on her books at zero dollars. Sometimes, however, tangible assets are depreciated only until they reach scrap value.

While she may carry the forklift on her balance sheet at zero in the eighth year from purchase forward on her balance sheet, it may still run and have some market value, perhaps $8,000. This example shows how market value may sometimes differ from book value. If Jackie were then to sell the forklift for the $8,000, she would have to report a gain on the sale and would, at that point, increase her pretax income by the amount of the sale. The accounting process would be similar to selling inventory, which had been written off.

Different long-term assets have varying estimated useful lives. For example, a computer might have a five-year estimated useful life. Commercial real estate might have a longer useful life, say 39 years. While some IRS guidelines exist, there is often some gray area as to how quickly a business may expense the cost of long-term assets. Note that the portion of real estate that is allocated to the underlying land may not be depreciated, as land is deemed not to lose its value over time (for accounting purposes, anyway).

Remember that an expense is incurred when value is lost. A reasonable determination of the lost value must be calculated to reflect the decline in long-term asset values over time. As mentioned earlier, when we discussed the income statement, we ignored the impact that depreciation would have had on Jackie's Hardware Store. We will now make the appropriate adjustments. Let's start with Jackie's long-term assets. Recall that Jackie had $1,100,000 of real estate and related improvements. Of this amount, she attributes $140,000 to land, which may not be depreciated. While commercial real estate is generally deemed to have a 39-year estimated useful life, for purposes of this example, Jackie ascribes a 30-year estimated average useful life to the $960,000 allocated to the building and improvements. By using the straight-line method of equal annual installments, we determine that her annual depreciation associated with the gradual loss of value of her real estate is approximately $32,000 dollars. This figure is calculated by dividing $960,000 by 30 years.

Her equipment, furniture, and fixtures, however, have a much shorter estimated useful life, say five years. The $400,000 of book value attributed to these assets would consequently result in an $80,000 annual noncash expense associated with the gradual loss of value of these assets. This figure is simply calculated by dividing $400,000 of book value by 5 years.

Adding the annual depreciation expense from the real estate value decline of $32,000 to the depreciation expense associated with the reduction in worth of the equipment, furniture, and fixtures of $80,000 yields a total annual noncash depreciation expense of $112,000:

Depreciation Expense (building and improvements)	$ 32,000
Depreciation Expense (furniture, equipment, fixtures)	80,000
Total Depreciation	$112,000

Interestingly, the $112,000 depreciation expense actually exceeded her $110,000 pretax income figure, resulting in a $2,000 loss! Because Jackie no longer shows a profit on her income statement, she no longer has to pay the $33,000 tax bill! Oddly enough, Jackie's business showing a loss results in an *increase* in cash:

Pretax Income	$ 110,000
Depreciation Expense	−112,000
Pretax Loss *after* Depreciation	($2,000)
Taxes	~~$ 33,000~~

Remember, profitability and liquidity are not the same thing. You may be profitable but lack the immediate cash necessary to pay this week's payroll. Also, accelerating depreciation expenses can increase a company's cash on hand due to depreciation's tendency to increase noncash expenses, reducing pretax earnings and therefore lowering one's taxable income.

In Jackie's case, we assumed that she used the simplest form of depreciation, the straight-line method of equal annual installments of asset value expense. We also depreciated the full amount of her long-term assets. In many cases, we only depreciate the asset until its book value reaches scrap value. The difference between the original cost and the scrap value (if any) is the amount we may expense, which is called the "depreciable cost." The book, or carrying, value of any depreciating long-term asset at any given time is the original cost less the accumulated depreciation to date.

In some cases, similar assets may be grouped together under the straight-line method. An example may be computer and phone systems that are purchased at about the same time with comparable estimated useful lives. These phones and computers might have a five-year estimated useful life, and the depreciable cost would be expensed equally over this five-year time frame.

There are popular depreciation methods other than straight-line that provide a faster means of writing off, or expensing, tangible assets through depreciation. One popular alternative is the *double declining balance method*. The declining balance method expenses, or depreciates, assets at twice the rate that the straight-line method would—at least initially. Let's look at how the declining balance method would have impacted Jackie's depreciation for her equipment. Keep in mind that Jackie started with $200,000 of equipment on her balance sheet—her cost of acquiring the necessary gear to make her business run smoothly.

The estimated useful life of this equipment was deemed to be five years. Had we utilized the straight-line method, her annual depreciation expense would have been one-fifth, or 20 percent, of the original equipment cost. With the declining balance method, we double the 20 percent and expense 40 percent of the book value of the equipment in the first year from purchase. In Jackie's case, this would amount to $80,000! Her carrying value would then be lowered from $200,000 to $120,000 in only 12 months. In the second year, she would depreciate, or expense, 40 percent of the new book value of $120,000. So, in the second year, her depreciation expense would be reduced to $48,000, leaving her with a year-end book value of $72,000. Likewise in the third year, she'd depreciate $28,800 (40 percent of $72,000), resulting in a $43,200 book value at the end of the third year. Her fourth-year earnings' hit would only be about $17,300, 40 percent of the $43,200 book value at the year's beginning. So at the end of the fourth year, she would have only $25,900 of equipment value remaining on her books. In the fifth year, she'd expense, or depreciate, the remainder. In this example, we have not left a small amount attributable to any scrap value the equipment might provide and have assumed that the depreciable cost is the entire purchase price of the asset.

The *sum-of-the-year's-digits* method of depreciation results in a more accelerated write-off of assets than straight line, but less than the declining balance method. Under this method, annual depreciation is determined by multiplying the depreciable cost by a schedule of fractions. Remember that the depreciable cost equals the original cost less the salvage, or scrap, value. Each year's book value equals the original cost less any accumulated depreciation. For an asset that has an estimated useful life of five years, the years' digits are 5, 4, 3, 2, and 1. The sum of the digits equals 15, or 5 plus 4 plus 3 plus 2 plus 1. The amount of the annual depreciation starts with the largest digit,

5, divided by the sum of the digits, 15, multiplied by the depreciable cost. Each subsequent year's depreciation is computed by dividing the next highest digit by the sum of the digits, 15, and multiplying the result by the depreciable cost.

In other words, the first year's depreciation would be five-fifteenths of the depreciable cost, the second year's depreciation would be four-fifteenths, the third year's depreciation would be three-fifteenths, the fourth year's depreciation would be two-fifteenths, and the fifth year's depreciation would be one-fifteenth. After five years, the carrying value, or book value, would be reduced to scrap value, where it remains until the equipment is discarded or sold.

Another depreciation method is based on activity. The *activity depreciation method* bases the gradual loss of value not on time but rather on usage. Consider a machine that is supposed to be functional for 10,000 hours of operation. Let's imagine that the machine cost $110,000 and has an estimated scrap value of $10,000. The machine's total depreciable cost, using the activity method, would be calculated as $110,000 of original cost less $10,000 of scrap value divided by 10,000 estimated useful hours. This would result in a depreciation expense of $10 per hour. The business would expense the number of hours used each year times $10 per hour until the machine's book value reached its scrap, or salvage, value. If, for example, the company used the machine for 3,000 hours annually, the depreciation expense using the activity method would be $30,000 dollars for each of the first three years, and $10,000 dollars in the fourth (as the salvage value would have been reached).

The *units-of-production depreciation method* is very similar to the activity method of depreciation. Instead of dividing the depreciable cost by the number of hours utilized, one would instead divide the depreciable cost by the number of units the machine was expected to produce. If the machine in the example above were likely to generate 5,000 toys, then the annual depreciation expense would be based on the number of toys made by the machine each year. With $100,000 dollars of depreciable cost, the depreciation expense would be $20 per toy made during the year until the machine drops to its scrap value. Provided that 2,000 toys are made in the first year after the machine's purchase, $40,000 of depreciation expense would be recorded using the units-of-production method. Each subsequent year would generate depreciation of the number of toys produced multiplied by $20 of depreciation cost per unit. Once the salvage value is reached, the depreciation expense stops.

Units-of-time depreciation is similar to the units-of-production method. It is used to depreciate, or expense, equipment that is utilized in natural resource exploration, especially in cases where the asset's use varies annually. The number and length of projects that are expected to be completed by the asset is established, and the depreciable cost is reduced by the amount of the asset's life that is correlated to each job.

Composite depreciation simply applies one depreciation rate to an entire asset with components with different estimated useful lives. For example, a particular building might have a strong foundation and frame that may last 39 years while the electrical and plumbing systems have much shorter lives, say 20 years. A composite depreciation process would apply a single, weighted average useful life to the entire building. This composite useful life would then be utilized along with one of the depreciation rates mentioned above.

Sometimes companies own natural resources such as timber, water supply rights, coal or gold mines, or oil fields. These businesses, like others, seek to maximize value for their owners. But the assets they utilize to accomplish the same ends may be a bit more complicated, especially when considering how to account for them on the balance sheets of their respective owners. Depreciation for long-lived productive natural resources assets is handled slightly differently from the way other long-term assets are handled.

Like other long-term asset purchases, natural resource assets are initially recorded on a balance sheet at their original cost. Suppose that, after a time, a huge oil deposit is discovered under the ground. While the value of the property has obviously increased substantially, the carrying value remains the same and is expensed over the appropriate time frame. The incremental profitability will greatly benefit the income statement as the oil is extracted over time. The huge discovery does not warrant an immediate recognition of the increased value. It is important to realize this when evaluating a company's balance sheet, as the book value in this case may materially understate the asset's true worth (see "Net Present Value" in Chapter 6).

Conversely, a property that is purchased at a high price with the anticipation of oil or gold being on the property by a business that later finds the land lacking in the natural resource would expense the excess asset carrying value in the period in which the overstatement is discovered (see "Write-downs and Write-offs," below).

The gradual loss of value of an oil field that is being pumped empty is called "depletion." Much like depreciation, depletion represents the gradual loss of value of the oil reserve due to the process of emptying the oil. When oil is discovered, the amount contained in the field is estimated through highly sophisticated geological techniques. The length of time that the field will be productive is also estimated along with the price of oil and the cost its extraction. (Some fields require far more cost to access due to their depth, surrounding rock formation, and purity.) Once the estimated annual production stream is determined, the amount of value that is used up each year is said to be depleted, and the amount depleted is expensed in the year in which the value is lost until only the land value remains on the company's books. This is analogous to the units-of-production depreciation process.

EXPENSING VERSUS CAPITALIZING

If Jackie's kids, Sloan Falcon and Aristotle, are playing stickball in front of Jackie's Hardware Store and one of them hits the ball through her store's window, would the money spent installing a new window be considered a repair, which warrants an immediate expense on her income statement, or an improvement to the building and added to its value on the corresponding balance sheet category (real estate and related improvements) and expensed over time?

The answer depends on whether the expenditure adds value to the building or simply replaces *value that has been lost*. If Jackie installs new, double-pane, energy-efficient windows that improve the worth of the building in which her store resides, she would not *expense* the cost of the window installation. Instead, she'd *capitalize* the cost by adding it to the long-term asset category, Real Estate and Related Improvements, and depreciate the price over the estimated useful life of the asset.

Conversely, a simple window pane replacement, since it adds no further value to the building, would be immediately expensed, as *the value would have been lost*. She simply brought the building back to where it was before the damage was inflicted by her athletic children. Perhaps she might recover the cost over time through the kids' free labor if she had them stock shelves or sweep floors.

Expensing versus capitalizing is often a gray area. Companies have gotten into trouble by taking unreasonable liberties when discretion is warranted (see Chapter 11). Not only is it often difficult to determine whether or not a research project, for example, is creating long-term value, but management can easily get away with telling an auditor that a certain check written was related to said project. So not only is it difficult to ascertain which endeavors warrant a determination of long-term value creation, but it is also challenging to figure out unequivocally how expenditures should be allocated among projects and departments. Auditors have a tough job ferreting out fraud and must rely on management representations to a very large degree.

Consider at a check written from a business to a landscaping company. The proceeds may have been used to cut the lawn or plow snow, either of which would have been classified as maintenance and immediately expensed, as the value had been immediately lost. Alternatively, the work performed may have been to install a patio or to plant trees. In these cases, lasting value would have been created. Such lasting value would justify the capitalization of these payments and the associated depreciation of the expenditure over time. This analysis requires the examination of the check written in conjunction with the invoice provided by the contractor. Imagine the amount of work and detail needed to confirm the legitimacy of every transaction undertaken by a large corporation over an entire year! Consider the price tag of such an undertaking at Big Four accounting firm billing rates, which sometimes run up to $1,000 per hour!

WRITE-DOWNS AND WRITE-OFFS

As discussed, asset values, while initially listed on the balance sheet at their cost, often fluctuate in value. Sometimes, there is a dramatic reason as to why an asset's value drops precipitously. For example, if a large customer of Jackie's Hardware Store files for bankruptcy, there is little likelihood that she'll collect the money that she is owed in the form of a receivable. If a company's inventory consists of old eight-track tapes, there is almost no chance that the business will be able to sell them at their original cost.

Another situation in which an asset's value may be dramatically overstated is a failed development project. Imagine that a pharmaceutical company had been developing a cancer drug. For years, many millions of dollars of research, experimentation, and salaries had been paid. Because it was anticipated that a valuable asset would be created, the costs associated with the drug's development had been capitalized. The annual costs grew and were piled onto the prospective drug's asset class on the pharmaceutical company's balance sheet.

When it came time for testing the drug with the U.S. Food and Drug Administration (FDA), however, it was determined that the drug actually *caused* cancer. All of the money burned through the years of research efforts would then be determined to be wasted. In short, at the time of the failed FDA test, it would be established that the *value had been lost*. Once the value is deemed to have been lost, the entire amount of the prospective drug asset would be expensed.

When a company determines that a more appropriate, lower value should be assigned to an asset, the difference, or the excess carrying value, should be expensed. This process of expensing excess asset value is considered to be a *write-down*. The write-down procedure has the effect of reducing the value of the asset by the amount of the write-down while increasing expenses by the same figure in the period in which the write-down occurs. When the more appropriate new asset value is deemed to be zero and all of the asset's carrying value is determined to be excess, the process of writing down the value to zero is called a *write-off*.

Many of the problems faced by banks and other financial institutions in the late 2000s was caused by the realization that the assets on their books were no longer worth their full carrying value. As an increasing percentage of loans extended to individuals and corporations started to default, these banks had to realize that their balance sheets no longer accurately reflected a realistic picture of their financial health. The loans, generally originated by the financial institutions and carried at the full principal amount, were no longer likely to be paid in full. The result was a huge number of write-downs.

The dramatic loss in asset levels did not alleviate the banks' obligation to pay their own liabilities, though. The result was a direct hit to their net worth, as the full amount of liabilities was subtracted from a smaller asset base. Because banks are required to maintain a minimum equity level of 8 percent of assets to maintain good standing from a regulatory standpoint, many needed cash infusions in the form of equity. The additional paid-in capital, in many cases, came from the U.S. government, as private investment dried up for fear that even more write-downs might be necessary. While the financial system limped through the crisis in late 2008 and 2009, taxpayers wound up owning substantial percentages of many large banks through the needed paid-in capital injections to avoid further financial meltdowns. As of this writing, the banks have been able to repay much of the money as the crisis has eased.

6

FINANCE CONCEPTS AND TOOLS

OPERATING VERSUS CAPITAL LEASES

Businesses often seek to make monthly (instead of lump-sum) payments to acquire the use of long-term assets such as equipment. The business seeking the equipment is called the "lessee" while the company providing the equipment is called the "lessor." There are two ways to account for these monthly payments, depending on certain properties of the arrangement. The streams of payment for which the company is obligated are classified as either operating leases or capital leases.

When a lease is classified as an *operating lease*, the lease payments are treated as operating costs. The operating lease does not show up as debt on the company's balance sheet. Many businesses prefer operating leases, as they don't make the required stream of payments look like debt obligations.

When the payments are considered *capital leases*, on the other hand, the present value of the lease expenses is treated as debt, and interest is imputed on this amount and expensed on the income statement. Reclassifying operating leases as capital leases can increase the debt on a balance sheet significantly, especially in businesses that have substantial operating leases, such as airlines. A lease must be treated as a capital lease if it meets any of the following four conditions:

1. The lease life exceeds 75 percent of the expected life of the asset.
2. There is a transfer of ownership to the lessee at the end of the lease term.
3. There is an option to acquire the asset for a nominal price at the end of the lease term.
4. The present value of the lease payments, discounted at an appropriate discount rate (the firm's cost of capital at the time the agreement is reached), exceeds 90 percent of the fair market value of the asset.

The lessor uses the same criteria for determining whether the lease is a capital or operating lease and accounts for it accordingly. If it is a capital lease, the lease receivable is shown as an asset on the balance sheet, and the interest revenue is recognized over the term of the lease as paid.

From a practical standpoint, the difference between operating leases and capital leases is that ownership of the leased asset generally transfers to the lessee at the end of a capital lease. Capital leases are essentially the purchase of the asset (along with the recording of the asset on the balance sheet) along with the associated debt used for the purchase.

The asset gets depreciated during the lease term, and the debt is similarly amortized. Operating leases generally result in the ultimate return of the equipment. Operating leases allow the lessee to enter into a new lease at the end of the term for new equipment, keeping the company's operating tools relatively new.

A simple analogy is the purchase of an automobile versus the lease of one. With a purchase, you may buy the car for $20,000 and borrow the entire amount for a period of six years at 8 percent. The monthly payments would be $350.66 for each of the 72 months. A $20,000 addition would be made to the equipment category on the balance sheet, and a $20,000 liability would be recorded as well. Assuming that the vehicle's estimated useful life is six years and the straight-line depreciation method is utilized, one-seventy-second of the car's price, or $278, would be expensed monthly for the gradual loss of value of the asset. In addition, the portion of each payment that is allocated to interest expense is also deducted on the income statement for the cost of capital. This monthly figure starts at about $133 and declines as the principal amount of the debt is paid down. On the balance sheet, the carrying value of the car drops by $278 per month, and the vehicle loan is reduced by each payment's principal portion.

With an auto lease for a car with the same price tag, you may simply pay a monthly fee that is expensed on the income statement. The asset is actually purchased from the car dealership by a bank or other specialty finance company and is effectively rented to you. As you wouldn't own it, you wouldn't add an asset or liability to the balance sheet and would return the vehicle at the end of the lease term. You might have an option to buy the car at the time for the expected residual value, which is the amount the finance company expects the auto to be worth at the end of the lease. The amount of the payments would be calculated by the finance company by adding the expected loss of value during the lease term to an effective interest charge on the total funds provided. While you're paying just a monthly fee, the fee represents an interest payment like a capital lease, plus the value decline borne by the car's owner, the bank.

An operating lease by definition has no virtually free purchase option at the end of the term, and the asset will not have been fully depreciated. For this reason, operating leases are often shorter in term than are capital leases. You may be aware that car leases often run 36 months or so. The payments are lower than those of capital leases, as the full value of the auto isn't lost, and the finance company doesn't need to charge you the entire cost of the car—it expects to recoup much of the money expended for the purchase upon its later sale at the estimated residual value. This is why you're limited regarding the number of miles allowed and must maintain the auto's condition. If you don't, the financial institution will get less than the car's anticipated residual value at its eventual sale and will charge you fees to cover much of the difference.

It is important to note that both operating leases and capital leases are company obligations. A business that looks like its balance sheet has little leverage might be hiding future payment requirements by classifying them as operating leases. To find out, read the notes to financial statements in a company's annual report. They often contain a lot of detail about future lease obligations, including the potential impact that the conversion of operating into capital leases would have on the balance sheet.

SALE LEASEBACK TRANSACTIONS

Companies that seek to raise cash but have dubious credit or short operating histories often employ *sale leaseback transactions* to secure required capital. A sale leaseback is simply the process of selling a long-term asset like equipment to an investor. The monies received by the business from the sale, net of any preexisting secured debt on the asset, are pocketed for working capital needs. The asset—in this case, the equipment—is no longer owned by the company. The business then rents, or leases, the equipment back from the purchaser. Sale leasebacks generally require that the business seeking capital pay a high rate of return (sometimes exceeding 20 percent) to compensate the investor for the increased risk of default. Unlike the extension of a secured loan, the transfer of title of the asset is required to avoid a foreclosure process should a default occur. Sometimes the business retains the ability to repurchase the asset from the investor once the lease payments are made or at any time for a premium to the investor's purchase price.

Sale leasebacks are often an indication that a company is struggling financially. Instead of lending the cash to the business, the investor requires immediate ownership of the asset effectively being financed. Should the company file for bankruptcy, the investor generally maintains ownership of the asset. (There are exceptions if the asset is sold at a discount to its true value shortly prior to such a filing.) Keep an eye out for companies that employ this strategy—it is often considered a last resort. Be careful when considering extending unsecured payment terms to businesses in this condition.

NET PRESENT VALUE

Some assets on the balance sheet are easier to value than others. Recall that assets are initially recorded on the balance sheet at their original cost. But as a prospective investor in a business, wouldn't you like to know if there is a dramatic difference between book value and market value of the company's assets? Some assets may provide a projected stream of payments to the company that owns them. Examples include an unconsolidated foreign subsidiary or a partial ownership of a partnership or annuity stream from an insurance company. The payments might be predetermined or estimated over time. Obviously, the annuity stream from the insurance company is more easily forecast than the periodic dividends from the foreign subsidiary. In either case, however, the ultimate market value of the underlying asset is calculated based on assumptions of future cash flows. Since long-term assets are recorded at their original cost, this analysis will help a prudent investor better understand the true value of the equity of the business, both on the balance sheet and the future impact on the income statement.

Once the stream of future cash payments is determined based on best-guess assumptions, including a possible terminal value from the potential future sale of the income- generating asset, a current valuation of the payments expected to be received must be ascertained. In order to convert the future cash flow stream into today's currency, each future payment must be discounted. How much each payment is discounted is based on time and risk.

The longer in the future the expected payment is, the lower its value today. And the greater the risk that the expected payment will not be made, the lower its current worth. Jackie might determine that a prospective concrete company investment bears sufficient risk to warrant a 40 percent minimum rate of return, or hurdle rate. Each future payment requires its own risk assessment. The risk assessment results in a discount rate, which is the effective interest percentage that one would reasonably require to buy the future payment today. An annuity payment from a highly rated insurance company might only need a 6 percent discount rate, as the future payment's likelihood would be very high. An expected dividend payment five years from now from a foreign subsidiary that is in a politically unstable environment might require a 50 percent discount rate.

Keep in mind that discount rates might vary, even from the same source. A payment from the insurance company next year may be very likely, while a payment from the same concern five years from now may be dubious due to the insurance company's required balloon debt repayment in two years or an uncertain license renewal process four years from now. For companies that are sufficiently large to have public bonds outstanding of varying maturities, the appropriate discount rate may be ascertained by looking to the effective interest rate that the market is dictating via the bonds' trading prices. In other cases, individual risk assessments are required to calculate the appropriate discount rates necessary to reduce future payment amounts to reasonable current levels.

The current value of future projected cash flows that have been discounted based on time and risk is called the "net present value," or NPV. The NPV is the sum of each future payment's current worth. Let's look at two examples.

A business is owed six annual payments of $1 million each from a large insurance company, the first being a full year from the date of the balance sheet. The first two payments are likely to be paid, as reflected in the trading prices of other unsecured public debt owed by the insurance company of similar durations, which yield 5 percent. The last four of the payments are deemed to be more vulnerable to default, and the public markets consequently demand a higher yield on the longer maturities of 8 percent. The public bond yield to maturity may be established by adding the cash interest payments to any discount from par that will be realized, or gained, over time should the bonds be redeemed in full upon maturity. In other words, if the bonds trade at 90 percent of the face value of the obligation, then a buyer would receive not only the interest payments when they come due but also the additional 10 percent of face value (to total 100 percent) should the bonds be paid in full at maturity and not default. This additional 10 percent of face value received would be added to the interest payments received to derive a total yield to maturity in excess of the stated coupon, or interest rate (the converse also holds true if the bonds trade at a premium to par). This total rate of return needs to be calculated in order to assess the market's view of the company's risk profile so that an appropriate discount rate may be established to determine the net present value of the future expected payments. Let us assume that this process has led us to believe that the previously mentioned 5 and 8 percent cost of the insurance company's capital are appropriate for assessing the value of the six annual annuity payments.

The first two payments of $1 million each (on the first and second anniversaries of the balance sheet date) may be valued as follows. Since you would need a 5 percent rate of return for one or two years from today to justify purchasing these future payments, we will need to "back up" to lower numbers. These lower numbers are the prices we would pay today to get $1 million in a year and in two years. In short, what number multiplied by 105 percent results in $1 million in a year? What number multiplied by 105 percent and again by 105 percent results in $2 million in two years? The answer to the first question is calculated by dividing $1,000,000 by 1.05, resulting in a net present value of the first payment of $952,381. Conversely, $952,381 multiplied by 5 percent interest, plus the original principal, yields $1,000,000. So the net present value of the first $1 million payment a year from now has been determined.

The second payment's current value is arrived at in the same fashion. One million dollars, discounted at 5 percent for two years, equals $1,000,000 divided by 105 percent, and the result is again divided by 105 percent. In number form, $1,000,000/1.05/1.05 = $907,029. So the second annual payment is worth $907,029 today.

The third through sixth scheduled payments are valued in the same manner, but a discount rate of 8 percent instead of 5 percent is used. Because the time frame is longer and the interest rates are higher, the subsequent payments are worth less today than the first two. The process by which we value the last four payments is laid out as follows:

Payment 3: $1,000,000/1.08/1.08/1.08 = $793,832

Payment 4: $1,000,000/1.08/1.08/1.08/1.08 = $735,030

Payment 5: $1,000,000/1.08/1.08/1.08/1.08/1.08 = $680,583

Payment 6: $1,000,000/1.08/1.08/1.08/1.08/1.08/1.08 = $630,170

So the total net present value of the six payments due from the insurance company is summarized below:

Payment	Payment Amount	Time in Future	Present Value
1	$1,000,000	One Year	$ 952,381
2	$1,000,000	Two Years	907,029
3	$1,000,000	Three Years	793,832
4	$1,000,000	Four Years	735,030
5	$1,000,000	Five Years	680,583
6	$1,000,000	Six Years	630,170
Total	$6,000,000		$4,699,025

The net present value of the $6,000,000 in future payments from the insurance company is worth only about $4,700,000 today.

Most firms are valued based on their ongoing cash flow and profits, not the liquidation value derived from selling the company's assets. For this reason, a similar exercise may be undertaken to value the entire company. (Net present value applies equally well to a single asset on a company's balance sheet or the business as a whole.) You may have heard of companies being valued on a price/earnings ratio (P/E), or multiple of annual net income. The P/E ratio, based on current earnings, is really a shortcut to a more comprehensive net present value calculation. A higher earnings growth rate normally results in a higher P/E ratio. This is simply due to the fact that higher anticipated future earnings streams, while discounted, still result in greater current values because the future amounts being discounted start bigger.

A company whose stream of expected earnings is likely to remain flat essentially forever with a high degree of confidence might have a discount rate to value the future income of 12 percent. In this case, the price to earnings multiple would be 1/.12, or 8.33. This calculation is a shortcut. A fixed stream of payments with a consistent risk profile may be present valued by dividing the amount of the annual payment by the appropriate discount rate: annual payment/discount rate. This formula provides the same result as adding together each future discounted annual payment using the same discount rate.

Companies with growing (or simply changing) anticipated income over time require a more comprehensive analysis of each year's earnings expectation and the appropriate discount rate to apply to each of the future income amounts (as though they were annuity payments). On a per-share basis, the value is calculated in the same fashion, but it is important to take into account the number of shares that a company might issue in the future. Stock grants to employees might dilute the ownership of the other shareholders without a clear justification to increase projected income as a result. On the other hand, issuing equity to purchase other businesses with incremental cash flow and profits may augment future earnings. Properly done, earnings per share will increase also. See "Using Equity as Currency" in Chapter 7 for more information.

It is important to factor in the number of shares outstanding when considering an earnings-per-share analysis. The tricky part comes in when there are dilutive securities outstanding, like warrants or convertible preferred stock. These instruments, upon conversion into common shares, will dilute the existing shareholders' ownership percentage. The extent to which such a conversion would be viewed as dilutive depends on whether or not the conversion price (for the convertible preferred stock) or strike price (for the warrants) is higher than the current trading price of the stock. If, for example, a warrant to purchase shares has a strike price of $15 per share and the stock is trading at $8 per share, the warrants would not be included in the fully diluted share figure. If the warrants had a strike price of $10 per share and the stock was trading at $20 per share, then the amount of shares that the warrants were able to buy at that price would be included in the total number used as a denominator when calculating earnings per share. The amount that would be received to buy the shares from the "in the money" warrant holder upon exercise would be added to paid-in capital.

As a shareholder, what is important to you is how much of a company's net income is your portion. A business that has dramatically higher income but issues many new shares to others may see earnings per share decline. The net income is the numerator; the number of shares is the denominator. Both count equally when determining share value. See "Accretive versus Dilutive Equity Transactions" in Chapter 7 for more details.

CAPITAL EXPENDITURES

As mentioned, the purchase of tangible long-term assets such as equipment is not an immediate expense because the value is not lost. The process simply transfers one asset, cash, to another asset, equipment.

But just because their purchase is not an expense on the income statement doesn't mean that you don't need to have the available resources for their ongoing acquisition. *Capital expenditures* include the purchase of, or upgrade of (remember capitalizing versus expensing?), fixed assets, including equipment, property, or real estate. These long-term assets are often critical in maintaining an efficient and competitive business. The purchase of these items does not show up as an immediate expense on the income statement, so even a profitable company may not be able to fund capital expenditure needs adequately. Aging vehicles or equipment might be a sign that cash is tight at a construction business. A hotel chain that has dated bedspreads or worn carpets may be having trouble paying debt service. Underfunding capital expenditures may bridge a short-term funding gap, but it reduces competitiveness over time. You'll probably overlook slightly dated hotel amenities once or twice; you probably won't return if shoddy conditions worsen (unless the price drops considerably as the establishment's reputation erodes). Maintaining assets is generally cheaper than discounting to compensate customers for declining service quality.

CASH FLOW

What exactly is cash flow? *Cash flow* is a generic term used differently, depending on the context. Loosely speaking, it shows how much money a company is able to generate for lenders, shareholders, or both after paying direct expenses and necessary overhead to operate the business.

Recall that operating income represents gross profit less operating costs. From the bottom up, operating income may also be described as earnings before (the impact of) interest and taxes (and other nonoperating costs), or EBIT for short. EBIT is a reasonable gauge to assess a company's ability to support debt service payments with any remainder available to equity owners.

There is no consideration for asset or liability changes in the EBIT figure, other than the fact that depreciation and amortization have already been subtracted. This is an important point. Remember that depreciation registers the amount that a company's equipment, for example, has lost value. This equipment needs to be periodically replaced! So it is important to factor in what we'll consider depreciation to be: a loosely labeled asset replacement reserve. EBIT does not factor in other balance sheet changes, like growth in accounts receivable or inventory. It is up to a company's management to oversee working capital and to keep current assets and current liabilities in reasonable harmony. This is done by making sure payment terms are extended only to creditworthy customers, to avoid writing down accounts receivable as a bad debt expense. If the company is growing and accounts receivable and inventory needs are also increasing, then management must find ways to finance the cost of the increased current asset needs. This may be done via cooperative vendors that allow longer accounts payable terms or through short-term borrowings through a line of credit secured by the larger current asset base.

EBIT provides the tools to handle long-term stuff. Sufficient EBIT enables long-term borrowings, which can be used to purchase long-term assets like equipment or real estate. Ample EBIT allows the paydown of debt obligations and provides return for shareholders.

Sometimes also referred to as cash flow, EBITDA—earnings before interest, taxes, depreciation, and amortization (and other nonoperating items)—is a desperate person's EBIT. EBITDA is simply EBIT plus the noncash portion of a company's expenses added back. I call EBITDA a desperate person's EBIT because it does not put aside the operationally necessary asset replacement reserve via depreciation consideration. In other words, a business may use EBITDA to service debt in the short run. If annual depreciation expense is not reinvested into property, plant, and equipment assets, though, the quality of the company's products or services will decline over time as the productive assets age. Businesses that are dependent on having quality, long-term assets to facilitate efficient operations that overleverage (i.e., borrow too much), based on the expectation that EBITDA is always available for debt service, often default on the debt. EBITDA also fails to reflect the inherent use of cash that occurs when a business grows and its level of accounts receivable increases. It is critically important to factor in balance sheet changes in conjunction with the income statement to evaluate a company's true financial health.

An example is the leveraged buyout of several Atlantic City casinos. By using EBITDA as the measurement of how much debt could be supported by the gaming operations, the companies were stripped of their ability to reinvest in hotel rooms, decor, and facilities. Even the felts on card tables were subsequently replaced so infrequently that they were notoriously stained and dirty. The result was that customers moved to newer facilities. Given that EBITDA then declined at the debt-strapped competitors due to loss of market share, several gaming concerns were unable to make the crippling debt service payments and filed for bankruptcy to restructure their balance sheets. Adding liabilities always increases risk, but when future payment assumptions are based on using capital expenditure funds for debt service, the danger escalates. Any hiccup in business from economic downturns exacerbates the risk.

Free cash flow, on the other hand, is the amount of money a business generates *after* paying for long-term asset investments. Defined as EBITDA less capital expenditures, free cash flow provides a much more accurate picture of how much cash a company's operations legitimately generate. Of course, evaluating the long-term assets a company has will help determine how much funds are likely to be needed in the short term. For this reason, projected free cash flow (based on reasonable assumptions) is the best barometer to assess a company's cash generation capabilities. Operating income on the profit and loss statement is generally higher than free cash flow because the regular purchase of necessary operating assets are not immediately expensed. Don't be fooled into thinking that the owners of a business have that cash available, though—debt service as well as short-term and long-term asset additions take first priority. When investors make this mistake and rob the business of the funds required for these items, a company's viability may be jeopardized.

LIABILITIES SUBJECT TO COMPROMISE

If a company files for bankruptcy, there is a strong likelihood that its creditors will not be paid in full. Upon such a filing, the "best interests of creditors" test is performed. The best interests test determines whether a sale of all of the company's assets should be pursued, with the proceeds paying off creditors in their respective priorities. If a liquidation is expected to generate less value than a restructuring of the business's balance sheet, then the company is reorganized as a going concern and continues to operate.

Typically, secured creditors (with collateral backing their claims) are paid first from the proceeds of a liquidation of the assets backing their loan. Any deficiency, or shortfall, may leave the balance of the debt to be lumped in with other unsecured creditors. An example might be a car loan. The sale of the car may provide only enough cash to pay part of the obligation, as the car's value may have declined below the outstanding loan amount. Only secured loans continue to accrue interest (up to the value of the underlying collateral) during a bankruptcy process.

In a restructuring, a company's projected income is determined in order to establish how much debt the business is able to support. Unsecured creditors, whose claims against the bankrupt company (i.e., the debtor) are in jeopardy of not being paid, are recategorized as a current liability titled "liabilities subject to compromise." The liabilities subject to compromise often wind up with new loans that have a longer payout period and/or a smaller face amount than their "prepetition" (before bankruptcy petition filing) claims plus a portion of the company's ownership. The amount of the reduction in their loans will determine how much of the business they will own after the reorganization. The previous owners' stake will be reduced, or diluted, by the equity granted to the creditors. In many cases, the prepetition equity is wiped out entirely.

Sometimes, an investor may purchase securities in a company that is likely to be reorganized or liquidated. In this case, the buyer (sometimes referred to as a "vulture investor") will seek to acquire the debt securities (bank debt, bonds, or vendor "trade" claims) at a significant discount to the claim amount owed by the debtor. The vulture investor then determines what the liquidation value of the assets might be, keeping in mind that the process of liquidation is costly. Companies that dispose of inventory often take as much as a 50 percent commission for the disposition process. Selling a house, which might be listed on the balance sheet at cost, would require a 5 percent selling fee to a real estate agent plus legal fees. A paid trustee often oversees the disposition of assets to maximize the recovery to creditors. In short, the company's asset book values may be reduced, or haircut, to compensate for the liquidation expenses. These costs must be factored in to determine how much money (i.e., how much of a discount) a vulture investor would be willing to pay to achieve an acceptable rate of return.

For example, let's look at a business with book values of $500,000 of cash, $1 million of inventory, $1 million of accounts receivable, and

$2 million of real estate. There are $5 million of liabilities, $2.5 million of which is a mortgage on the real estate. The property may be sold for $2 million less 5 percent in expenses, leaving $1,900,000 of net value from the disposition of the real estate. Since the mortgage had a first lien on the property that has not been satisfied, the mortgage holder would receive all of these proceeds. The difference, or $600,000, would be lumped together with the unsecured creditor pool, leaving a total of $3.1 million of total unsecured liabilities to share equally (or "pari passu") the liquidation proceeds of the remaining assets. If the liquidation trustees fees are estimated to be $300,000, there would be $200,000 of cash remaining. Adding this remaining cash ($200,000) to the 50 cents on the dollar realized from the distressed sale of the inventory ($500,000, half of the book value) and 80 percent recovery realized on the accounts receivable ($800,000, or 80 percent of $1 million—customers are less likely to pay a liquidating vendor) leaves $1.5 million of ultimate liquidation proceeds. This $1.5 million must be shared among the $3.1 million in total unsecured claims, resulting in a 48 percent recovery at some point in the future. In order to make a sufficient profit and to justify the wait until getting paid as well as the possibility that the claim pool rises (increasing the denominator) through subsequent claim declarations, the vulture might offer to pay prepetition unsecured creditors 25 cents on the dollar. Equity holders would then be wiped out.

In the case of a reorganized company, the value of the pie does not come from the disposition of the business assets. To the extent that the company can continue to operate as a going concern while paying its daily expenses with something left over for stakeholders such as lenders and shareholders, the recoveries are generally much higher for all. In this case, projected income statements and balance sheets must be created using "reasonable" assumptions. ("Reasonable" assumptions often include ridiculous notions such as revenue will double every month forever.) Companies generally underperform the expectations set by such forecasts. However, they are the basis for determining what a business is worth (most importantly: is it worth more to the most senior impaired creditor class as a going concern or in a liquidation?), how much debt it can afford to pay going forward, and what kind of profit will be left for postpetition shareholders in the reorganized company. If the projections are too optimistic and the new (even reduced) debt load is too cumbersome based on overly rosy anticipated financial results, another restructuring may await down the road.

The new, postpetition debt's value is based on whether the stated interest rate compensates for the risk factoring in reduced overall leverage and the likelihood that projected cash flows will enable the business to repay the obligations from operations or enable the refinancing of the debt. Assuming that the market views the newly issued debt in the reorganized company to be worth par, or 100 cents on the dollar, any excess value would be allocated to the new preferred shareholders and then to common stockholders. Keep in mind that the restructured debt and equity on the postpetition balance sheet are generally owned in different proportions. Those are based on the seniority of the stakeholders before the modifications and the extent to which the overall enterprise value is deemed to exceed the postpetition debt.

When Chrysler and General Motors went through the bankruptcy process in 2009, however, supposedly pari passu (legally equal in seniority) creditors were, in my view, not treated equally. Union claims were given precedence over financial investors like banks and bondholders. It is my opinion that General Motors bondholders were thrown under the proverbial bus (trading at about 5 percent of claim upon filing), while supposedly equal union retirement claims were nearly made whole, according to Reuters.[1] I wish that I could offer a reasonable justification for this lack of justice but I can't. I'd urge you to stay away from investments in which the U.S. government controls the outcome because you don't know what the rules are.

Many companies were acquired using lots of leverage in the era of easy money. In other words, the purchase prices were largely borrowed. The lenders accepted the projections put forth at the time to issue loans to help pay the shareholders of the businesses that were sold. Unfortunately, while the acquired companies subsequently may generate positive operating profit, the cash flow has often been insufficient to cover the interest expense of the newly issued debt. For example, Harrah's Entertainment, the gaming giant, which was acquired by Apollo Management and TPG Capital for $31 billion in January 2008, saw the trading price of some of its debt obligations plummet to as low as 15 cents on the dollar a little more than a year after the company was sold according to Bloomberg.[2] Trying to avoid bankruptcy due to the enormous debt load, according to *BusinessWeek*, the company has sought debt exchange offers with bondholders.[3] Such offers often include partial principal forgiveness and maturity extensions in exchange for a greater interest rate, a higher position in the capital structure, or both, increasing the likelihood that the bonds will receive at least a partial recovery should the company file for bankruptcy. Of course, such a "leapfrog" move may cause other creditors to lose their relatively senior status in the capital structure, and the moves may be contested. Special treatment or beneficial transactions for a certain creditor within three months (one year for insiders) prior to filing Chapter 11 may be viewed by a bankruptcy judge as a "preference payment."

Obviously, those businesses that carry high debt loads relative to their ability to generate cash flow are most susceptible to bankruptcy. The pressure to meet interest and debt payments often leads to the underfunding of equipment purchases, inability to take advantage of bulk inventory acquisition, and delaying the upgrading of plants or facilities. Companies that do such things often were purchased with borrowed funds. In other words, the monies that are owed to creditors were used to pay the selling shareholders. This is a very different use of debt than borrowing money to buy an asset like a truck, forklift, building, or copy machine. These assets help make a company's operations more efficient and generate a return on the investment. The process of buying a company using substantial debt and little equity capital is called a "leveraged buyout," or LBO. LBOs saddle acquired businesses with heavy debt service burdens without the tangible assets to support operations.

This financing of goodwill (purchase of a company for more than its tangible assets) using debt is a risky proposition in itself. In addition, lenders are often induced to make such loans based on optimistic projected income statements. When and if the businesses do not meet these expectations, insufficient cash flow remains after direct and operating costs to pay debt service while simultaneously covering capital expenditure requirements. In addition, the sale of liquidated tangible assets is then insufficient to cover obligations owed due to the extensive goodwill on the post-acquisition balance sheet. Goodwill may not be amortized. When its value is clearly impaired, however, it may be written off. When a business fails and its tangible assets are liquidated, there is no longer any value to its goodwill.

CONTINGENT LIABILITIES

A *contingent liability* is one that a business needs to pay only when certain circumstances occur, such as losing a lawsuit or another firm defaulting on debts that have been guaranteed by the business. If Jackie's Hardware Store is being sued for $1 million by mesothelioma patients for historically selling asbestos-laden insulation, she might "win" in court over time or lose the case and owe $1 million. How does she account for this potential claim?

With guidance from her attorneys about the probabilities of different outcomes, a weighted average cost is determined, and a reserve is established to absorb the future cost. Let's say that her professionals calculate that there is an 80 percent chance of an ultimate dismissal of the case with zero liability and a 20 percent chance of a judgment against her business for the full $1 million. In this situation, Jackie would establish a reserve of $200,000, the expected value of the claim against the store. This is calculated by multiplying the $1,000,000 exposure times the 20 percent chance that it occurs. Jackie would have to take a $200,000 expense against earnings in the period in which the claim's value is determined.

As the case moves through the courts, her probabilities may change due to different rulings, and the reserve amount may be modified accordingly. Additional reserves would result in additional charges against earnings. Reduced reserve requirements would essentially add back to earnings the portion of the reserves that are no longer deemed necessary at the time the reserve is considered excessive. Once the reserve is established, Jackie no longer has to take a hit against earnings to settle the case for a value less than the reserved amount. For this reason, she always wants to keep this figure confidential; its disclosure provides the plaintiffs with powerful information as to how much Jackie can afford to pay without further earnings pain.

Other contingent liabilities arise when a company stands behind, or guarantees, the liabilities of another business or individual. If the other party defaults, the guarantor faces a claim equal to the full amount of the liability being guaranteed. This form of contingent liability is actually quite similar to the lawsuit analysis above. If Jackie had wanted to help her sons start their own business but they did not have sufficient credit or assets to get a loan, she may have offered a $100,000 guarantee from Jackie's Hardware Store. Jackie's Hardware Store determined that there was a 30 percent chance of default on the $100,000 guarantee. Consequently, Jackie recorded a $30,000 expense in order to provide a reserve against the contingent liability from the guarantee.

When her sons are more established and are able to refinance the loan without Jackie's Hardware Store's guarantee, Jackie may then reverse the reserve and benefit from a pretax earnings hike when the guarantee is effectively extinguished. Enron provided substantial debt guarantees to affiliated partnerships. According to *Bloomberg*, American International Group actually sold insurance to protect against others' corporate defaults, receiving premiums and paying certain liabilities of companies like Lehman Brothers and General Motors when the obligors failed to honor their debts.[4]

Insurance companies are experts at contingent liability analysis (although isn't AIG an insurance company?) Their primary business is to evaluate the merits of claims and to establish appropriate reserves against the liabilities. On the flip side, they receive monthly premiums and invest the money to prepare for future obligations. Many claims are settled, and insurance companies generally try to pay out less than the reserve amounts on their balance sheets. In this fashion, each claim that is effectively settled at a discount actually increases earnings because a larger payout had been expected. Spending less helps increase income just like increasing revenue.

I can't talk about contingent liabilities without discussing the U.S. government. Uncle Sam, through increasing spending levels for decades, has "lost" money almost every year. This accumulated deficit has been financed through increased borrowings. The government's debt now exceeds $12 trillion (yes, with a "T"), at least on the government's "balance sheet." According to the Congressional Budget Office, it is projected that another $1 trillion to $2 trillion of debt will be added each year to cover the continued shortfall between tax receipts and spending.[5]

While these figures are staggering, of additional concern are the incremental contingent obligations, both implicit and explicit, that the U.S. government maintains. Worse, these guarantees (or the theoretically associated reserves) are not included in the debt figures listed above. In 2008, the implicit government guarantees of the $5 trillion (yes, another T) in Fannie Mae and Freddie Mac debt obligations were made explicit, according to *Bloomberg*.[6] In my opinion, there is no longer a "maybe" about whether or not the taxpayers are on the hook. Yes, there is collateral supporting a portion of the Fannie and Freddie debt (pools of mortgages originated with lax underwriting standards), but real estate values have plummeted since then. Certainly, some reserves are appropriate. Maybe it is easier to pump another $50 billion or $100 billion at a time into these firms whenever needed. By doing so, the guarantees are never officially called but the pain is still imposed on taxpayers.

In my view, any cuts to any program alienates some constituency. For example, proposing to raise the retirement age (currently 62 or 65 years of age) for people to start to collect Social Security angers senior citizens (even though the American expected life span at birth has risen from 59 years in 1930 to roughly 79 years today). In other words, it seems as if we're getting paid for a larger and larger percentage of our expected lifespans. Maybe someday we'll live to be 130 years of age and spend most of our lives living off of the government dole. Cutting welfare benefits upsets the poorer folks. Reducing illegal alien protections, like health care and tuition assistance, hurts the minority vote. It is my opinion that politicians, fearful of alienating any group, make decisions accordingly in order to get reelected. When they do that, virtually every major spending bill gets approved (along with the associated ugly pork for the special interest groups), and our country's long-term fiscal stability wanes.

While monetary and spending reform is still theoretically possible, our politicians seem to view any spending program as forever written in stone. Consequently, the future payments the government makes related to entitlements are effectively contingent liabilities (with a nearly 100 percent chance of requiring funding). For we will never not honor Social Security payments. We will certainly provide Federal Deposit Insurance Corp. (FDIC) coverage to people whose bank fails. (According to the *Wall Street Journal*, the FDIC, at the time of this writing, had a negative balance and was preparing the "mechanics" for borrowing from the U.S. Treasury.)[7] I believe the United States will always find money for welfare checks and Medicare payments. We will continue to pay interest on our gigantic debt load. How? We will print more dollars, decreasing their individual value.

Our next agenda item will be to put the knowledge gained so far to practical use.

7

BALANCE SHEET UTILIZATION AND IMPLICATIONS

USING EQUITY AS CURRENCY

Sometimes companies seek to preserve cash by utilizing pieces of owner-ship to motivate employees, acquire assets, or purchase other businesses. By doing so, the company dilutes existing ownership stakes by the amount of new equity that is issued in these transactions. Presumably, having a stake in the success of the business will motivate employees to perform better. Whether this is true or not is subject to debate, but the practice often allows organizations to reduce the amount of required cash to retain top talent. The amount expensed for such issuance is based on the number of shares issued and the trading price of those shares at the time of issuance.

Another use of equity is for the acquisition of another business. Sometimes this is accomplished by a private business issuing a portion of its shares, membership interests, or partnership interests to another company's owners in exchange for ownership interests of the business being purchased; other times, just the assets of the target company are acquired.

Solely buying a company's assets carries much less risk than a stock purchase. When a company's stock is purchased, the assets as well as liabilities come along with the deal. To the extent that the new owner is clearly informed about all of the liabilities that are obligations of the business, the transaction is fair to both parties. Buying stock allows the purchaser to acquire a bigger company due to the effective leverage utilized in the purchase. Only the equity needs to be bought, and the assets are effectively financed by the existing liabilities on the balance sheet of the business being purchased. There is always a risk that the liabilities are greater than anticipated, however. Imagine that fraud has hidden the true obligations of the company being acquired. After the deal is done, the purchaser may feel buyer's remorse in part due to claims surfacing that were unanticipated. Such claims may originate through vendor invoices that were never recorded, taxes that were never paid, or litigation related to the company's past practices.

A good example is the taint experienced by companies that acquired asbestos manufacturing businesses years ago. Even though those claims arose long after the deals were closed, class action lawsuits cost the acquiring companies billions of dollars of medical expenses, higher insurance premiums, settlement costs, and of course, legal fees. Because the dangers (and corresponding liabilities) associated with the asbestos in the insulation products that were produced was not yet known, the companies that bought the equity of other businesses in this field were blindsided.

The purchase of assets, on the other hand, is safer. When bought properly, assets come unencumbered by liabilities. Does an asset purchase completely protect a buyer from a later lawsuit? Of course not. But one's defenses are much, much stronger. Equity holders are by definition subordinate, or junior in right of payment, to liability holders (creditors) in a business. And while new owners may insist on indemnification, or protection from sellers, for potential but undisclosed prior liabilities, chasing them later is a difficult and costly process.

Whether a public company buys assets or equity of another business, many transactions are effected utilizing the stock of the buyer to compensate the owners of the selling business for the ownership of the company being acquired. For the buyer, the amount of ownership in its business that is issued to the selling shareholders determines whether or not the potential acquisition makes economic sense.

ACCRETIVE VERSUS DILUTIVE EQUITY TRANSACTIONS

In any business decision utilizing company resources, management must ascertain whether or not an asset purchase makes the most sense for its owners. This is true on a micro or macro level. A corner Laundromat, for example, may have $1,000 to spend on either a snack machine or another dryer. General Electric may, for example, have had the wherewithal to purchase a company like Telemundo, the Spanish-speaking network to complement its National Broadcast Company (NBC) investment (prior to selling NBC to Comcast). Or GE might instead invest in a power plant on a barge off the coast of Nigeria or develop a new health-care technology. No business has unlimited resources, and those managers who allocate company assets are to be held responsible for the decisions they make. Each transaction directly affects individual shareholders.

If you own 10 percent of a company that earns $1 million per year, your share of the business income will be $100,000 annually. If the management enters into an agreement that results in your $100,000 increasing to $150,000 each year, you as an owner will be thrilled! Such a transaction is considered *accretive,* because it increases earnings per share. On the other hand, if management makes a deal that reduces your income to $50,000 next year, you won't be quite so pleased. A transaction that reduces earnings per share is considered *dilutive* to shareholders.

Imagine that the ABC Corporation is a publicly traded C corporation. ABC has one million shares outstanding that trade on the New York Stock Exchange at $20 each. ABC's market capitalization is then said to be $20 million. This is calculated simply as 1,000,000 shares outstanding times the $20 price per share. ABC Corporation earns $1 million per year and therefore has earnings per share of $1.00. Again, the math is straightforward: $1,000,000 of profit divided by 1,000,000 shares outstanding equals $1.00 per share.

XYZ Company, a private company with no public float or shares available for purchase on a stock exchange, also earns $1 million per year. XYZ is for sale for $10 million. ABC Corporation agrees to buy XYZ for the full asking price of $10 million utilizing shares of ABC stock. In order to come up with the purchase price, ABC issues 500,000 shares of stock, worth $20 apiece, to the owners of XYZ Company. This is calculated as 500,000 shares times $20 per share equals the $10,000,000 sought by the XYZ shareholders.

Was this a good decision by the managers of ABC Corporation? The answer lies in whether or not the transaction was accretive or dilutive to ABC shareholders. Let's look at the pro forma results (i.e., assuming that the transaction had already occurred). ABC Corporation's earnings have now increased from $1 million prior to the transaction to $2 million annually due to XYZ's additional $1 million of net income that now benefits ABC. ABC Corporation has more shares outstanding, though, and consequently has more hands to share in the increased earnings. ABC had one million shares prior to the deal getting consummated, but now it has another 500,000, with a new total of 1.5 million shares outstanding. Dividing the new total earnings of $2,000,000 by the revised shareholder base of 1,500,000 shares equals $1.33 per share. In short, the transaction has increased ABC's earnings per share by one-third, from $1.00 to $1.33; it is therefore accretive and desirable. Good job, ABC management!

Different types of buyers may offer better value for equity holders of companies for sale. Obviously, if you own some or all of a business and you wish to liquidate your interests, you would like to get as much as possible for your investment. Consider the varying categories of business purchasers in the marketplace and their differing interests.

Let's look at a local, singular grocery store for sale. It generates a certain amount of revenue and profit and seeks a reasonable asking price, as its owners are looking to move on to other ventures or to retire.

Clearly, any company buyer seeks to get more money in the future than it invests today. Financial investors that buy equity in businesses include individuals, pension funds, insurance companies, hedge funds, and mutual funds. These institutions make investments on their own behalf or for others. Their objective is to realize a profit through appreciation in the value of the shares or other assets they buy. The financial investor may consider purchasing a small grocery store as an investment. In doing so, based on current income levels, the return on investment might be 20 percent. (The purchase price in this case is expected to be five times net income, so the return is one-fifth of the purchase price, or 20 percent.)

Strategic investors include vendors, customers, or competitors. Just like financial investors, strategic investors look to make a profit on investments on behalf of their owners. A strategic investor, a large grocery store chain, is also considering the acquisition of the small, private grocery store. The large chain has advantages over the financial investor, however. Because it already buys from suppliers a lot of similar inventory (e.g., fruit and vegetables, meat and poultry, paper products, dairy products, canned goods, and other stocked items), it is able to extract concessions from vendors that result in lower prices and better payment terms. The grocery store chain also has another store in the area, so its existing advertising coverage will allow it to eliminate the advertising expense for the smaller store after purchase. The larger competitor has an existing accounting department that can handle this function for the acquired store going forward, eliminating salaries for bookkeepers at the small store. And because less competition will exist in the area, the large grocery store chain may be able to raise prices at both stores. This combination of beneficial factors in a purchase by a strategic investor is called "synergy." Due to the synergies associated with the deal, the strategic investor in this case, the large grocery store chain, might realize a 40 percent return on its investment (through an effective doubling of net income) if the price were the same as that proposed by the financial investor. Alternatively, the chain might pay a premium to the financial investor's maximum purchase price and still derive a superior rate of return.

For these reasons, companies are generally better off looking for strategic buyers when looking to sell their business so that their owners realize maximum benefit.

IMPACT OF INFLATION ON THE BALANCE SHEET

Sometimes people view inflation as an evil process that depletes the value of hard earned savings. This is not always the case. Inflation is, quite simply, the decline in the purchasing power of the U.S. dollar (or whatever currency is utilized by the business). The type of assets held by an individual or business as well as the corresponding leverage employed will determine how favorable or unfavorable the impact inflation will have.

Certain assets lose value as domestic inflation rises. Examples are cash (in U.S. dollars) and accounts receivable. If a business holds U.S. dollars and the dollar weakens, more of the cash will need to be utilized to purchase the same amount of goods. Accounts receivable, similarly, lose value, as the cash to which they convert has reduced purchasing power upon receipt.

Other assets may increase in value with inflation. A company may own real estate or foreign currency, both of which would likely grow in value denominated in U.S. dollars. To exaggerate the point, imagine that an owned building is worth $1 million. Now let's drop the value of the U.S. dollar by 50 percent. Now it takes twice as many dollars to buy the building, which is currently worth $2 million. In short, hard assets offer greater protection from a falling local currency.

Imagine that the $1 million building is purchased with a $1 million loan, or mortgage. Should the U.S. dollar decline in value through inflation by 50 percent, the business now would have an asset worth $2 million but still owe only $1 million. One million dollars of value has been created through inflation. Yes, the $1 million is worth half of what it once was, because of the dollar's reduced purchasing power. But there is still $500,000 of pre-inflation dollar purchasing power that has materialized through sharp inflation. This is because liabilities do not rise with inflation (although interest rates often go up, making adjustable loans more expensive). So, if a company has significant debts along with substantial tangible long-term assets, its balance sheet is well poised to handle an inflationary period.

Of course, the impact on inflation must also be considered on the income statement. To the extent that inflation hurts business profits, the balance sheet will suffer as well over time due to lower retained earnings. The main determinant on the positive or adverse effect that inflation has on the income statement is whether the price received for goods or services sold rises faster or slower than a company's expenses. For example, if a restaurant is unable to raise prices in a competitive environment (like my favorite bastion of capitalism, the mall food court) and its costs for food inventory go up, its gross margins will be squeezed and its profitability will decline. Airlines are highly dependent on the price of jet fuel, which sometimes reaches 40 percent of their operating expenses. When the price of oil and jet fuel rise, airlines generally see profits fall because the industry has so many competitors and travelers tend to be very price sensitive through the utilization of the Internet for fare shopping. As mentioned in Chapter 2, some astute airlines have locked in long-term supply contracts for jet fuel during lower oil price environments. These businesses have been able to better weather the storm when jet fuel prices have skyrocketed, and some weaker competitors have been forced to enter bankruptcy to reorganize or liquidate.

Having hard assets like real estate utilizing liabilities that don't increase in dollar terms during an inflationary period is one way to protect oneself from inflation. If you are concerned about the potential for the United States to default on its enormous debt, don't be. That's because the U.S. government has the ability to print unlimited dollars to meet its obligations. The effect of such a process would be to render the dollar "diluted," much like having lots of extra shares issued in a company. Borrowing money now at long-term fixed rates to purchase tangible assets like real estate or commodities offers maximum equity value protection if you expect the dollar to fall (as I do). Investing in (loaning money for the purchase of) long-term U.S. government securities (bonds) that are not inflation protected or keeping cash may seem safe but still may result in a decline in the value of one's nest egg.

THE IMPACT OF CURRENCY FLUCTUATIONS ON A BALANCE SHEET

To the extent a business pays its expenses domestically in local currency and generates sales in the same country receiving the same currency as payment, the fluctuation of the U.S. dollar against the euro or the Japanese yen will have no direct impact on the company's financial statements. However, if your balance sheet assets and liabilities are listed in U.S. dollars and your company owns foreign assets or is obligated to repay debts in other currencies, foreign exchange rates may have a dramatic impact.

Let's say that banks in Japan are willing to lend money at 1 percent interest—this is not far from the truth. Your American business agrees to accept the loan but must repay it in Japanese yen. It should be easy to convert the money to U.S. dollars and generate a return on the money in excess of the 1 percent interest expense. This real strategy is called the "carry trade." Simply putting the cash into a domestic certificate of deposit should yield at least double the cost of capital, generating a profit. However, there is a risk that the dollar weakens in value relative to the yen, resulting in losses.

Imagine that the dollar buys 100 yen when the loan is issued. Let's say that the debt is 100 million yen, which gets immediately converted into 1 million dollars. Subsequently, the dollar's purchasing power declines (due to, say, a perception of increasing Japanese government financial strength and a limited yen supply versus the American government's declining fiscal prowess and growing number of dollars issued). Now the dollar may be traded for only 80 yen. In other words, you now need more dollars to pay off the obligation. Specifically, you'll now need $1.25 million to pay off the 100 million yen liability. The converse works as well. A strengthening dollar will make the debt easier to repay.

Companies with international operations constantly evaluate (and hopefully manage) the risks associated with currency fluctuation in the jurisdictions where they operate. Some large financial institutions offer businesses hedging contracts called "swaps." These are effectively insurance contracts that require premiums but compensate the holders if commodities, or in this case, currency exchange rates, change in value. If customers pay an American business in euros and the euro strengthens against the U.S. dollar, the company effectively benefits from a price increase proportional to the percentage increase. For example, a euro-denominated contract that is modestly profitable when a euro buys $1.25 will see a 20 percent effective price increase if costs remain flat and the euro purchases $1.50 when received. Since dollar expenses don't necessarily rise when this occurs, the extra 20 percent of revenue flows down to the operating profit line of the company. Of course, if the same business must pay expenses in euros as well, much of the benefit is eaten up with higher costs.

Exporters love a weak domestic currency. It makes it easier for their foreign customers to afford their products. For companies that purchase their goods abroad through importation, the opposite is true.

A strong U.S. dollar, for example, makes it easier for American companies (and consumers for that matter) to afford foreign goods and services. According to the Financial Times, China has been criticized for intentionally keeping the yuan artificially cheap; its value is fixed by the People's Republic against the dollar.[1] Doing so benefits the many exporters in the Asian nation. This is one reason, I believe, why U.S. citizens purchase so many Chinese-made goods—they're cheap relative to other things that may be purchased with a U.S. dollar. But their frequent purchase has led to hundreds of billions of dollars leaving the United States and caused an enormous trade deficit. China has used much of this inflow to lend money to the United States. In fact, the United States now owes China almost $1 *trillion*!

In government and industry, balance sheet utilization is often mismanaged. Some of the problems faced by executives in the pursuit of financial gain and representatives furthering flawed public policy will now be examined.

8

BALANCE SHEET ABUSES

LEVERAGE AND THE ERA OF EASY MONEY

There have been many instances in the past where borrowing too much has gotten companies into trouble. But in the latter part of 2008 there was an unbelievable revelation as to the extent to which it had become an obsession not only in the United States but also worldwide. Starting in the late 1990s and accelerating after September 11, 2001, the U.S. Federal Reserve had made easy money a priority to promote economic growth. Interest rates had remained at historic lows, and lending standards had become precipitously weak. Banks, competing to put cheap money to work, were so anxious to make loans that hundreds of billions of dollars of "no-doc" loans (short for "no documentation"; also affectionately called "liar loans") were underwritten, which required no income verification by the borrowers. These no-doc loans were easily resold to quasi-government agencies Freddy Mac and Fannie Mae, whose appetite was fueled by Congress wanting to make home ownership available to almost anyone.

Real estate appraisers were asked to rubber-stamp valuations that allowed refinancing of homes at multiples of their original cost. Banks were writing "cov-lite" loans to businesses (without the usual stipulations, or covenants, such as the borrower must remain profitable or maintain sufficient working capital). To make things worse, these dubious loans themselves were packaged together into pools and further leveraged!

The pools, or groups of similar mortgages and loans, were bundled together in complex packages called "structured investment vehicles" (SIVs), which were used as collateral for loans. Sometimes the amount of money lent to these SIVs approached or exceeded the face value of the loans in the pools. The remaining equity in the pools, along with some of the loans against the pools, sat on the books of some large institutions such as Bear Stearns and Lehman Brothers, two historical Wall Street powerhouses. Incredibly, the billions of dollars of loan pool assets on their balance sheets were used as collateral for *additional debt of as much as 40 times their stockholders' equity.* (Hey, why not use OPM—other people's money?)

So long as no significant defaults occurred and the real estate market continued to increase, these companies were able to generate huge profits relative to their stockholders' equity because they themselves were able to borrow money so cheaply. But after the real estate market peaked and started to decline, defaults started to rise, and the house of cards started to fall.

To make matters worse, some of the debt issued by many institutions, including Lehman Brothers, was extremely short term in nature. Typically, it is less expensive to borrow short-term funds than longer-term maturities because as the repayment period is extended, more uncertainty about future conditions brings greater risks to lenders, who generally charge higher interest rates. This condition is known as a "positive yield curve," where rates go up as maturities are extended.

The debt with extremely short maturities (often 30 to 90 days) sought by many firms is called "commercial paper." Commercial paper is often purchased by theoretically safe money market funds seeking short-term income. The risks to the companies were evident when credit markets started to dry up in late 2008 and the commercial paper was not easily refinanced. By trying to save a percentage point or so of interest expense, these businesses exposed their very viability to the whims of the short-term debt markets. Lehman's collapse occurred in part due to a loss of confidence that the company would be able to repay these loans. This belief became a self-fulfilling prophecy. Lehman's defaults nearly shut down the commercial paper market that so many firms had utilized. Exposure to Lehman's short-term debt resulted in at least one money market fund to "break the buck," or lose principal for its investors. Frightened, lenders realized that the small amount of interest received for these loans did not sufficiently compensate them for the previously underestimated risks. More defaults were likely.

Ultimately, the U.S. government stepped in (again) to guarantee *trillions* of dollars of commercial paper issuance to restore confidence in the instruments. With Uncle Sam's backing, money started to flow again, enabling businesses across all industries to continue to borrow to repay the short-term loans as they came due.

At the same time, the collateralized debt obligations' underlying mortgages, sometimes written with teaser rates of as low as 1 percent, with interest-only payments for a time, and representing nearly 100 percent of the price of the real estate at the peak of the market, began to wobble. As rates adjusted after the teaser periods, homeowners had more and more trouble making the payments. (Remember, many loans were so-called liar loans written based on drastically overstated income.) Foreclosures occurred. Banks now owning real estate put a large supply of REO (real estate owned) on the market at the same time. Other sellers, trying to compete with the banks' inventory overhang, had to drop prices, sometimes precipitously, to get rid of their property. People with mortgages that were now significantly underwater (i.e., the value of their mortgage well exceeded the value of their property) were walking away from their homes, handing the keys to the banks.

Delinquencies rose. The value of the loans declined, often to the point of wiping out the equity ownership in the leveraged mortgage pools and substantially haircutting (reducing the value of) the liabilities that were secured by the groupings. Many of these assets (the loans to and equity in the mortgage pools) fell by 50 percent in some cases in a very short time. The investment banks and hedge funds that had borrowed up to $40 for every $1 of equity on their balance sheets were suddenly insolvent. Insurance companies like AIG that had guaranteed some of the Lehman Brothers and Bear Stearns debts, lost their previously stellar (at least on the surface) credit ratings and were consequently required to post additional capital to their counterparties, which they could not afford to do. Washington Mutual, Merrill Lynch, Wachovia, and other major financial institutions were forced into the hands of relatively stronger partners. Freddy Mac and Fannie Mae fell into government conservatorship, and the U.S. banking industry melted down. Banks stopped lending to all but the most creditworthy clients, and economic growth turned negative.

Remember we talked about return on assets as well as return on equity? The difference is debt, or leverage. In order to boost return on equity, overly zealous managers borrowed aggressively to buy dubious assets when credit was cheap. Imagine a business that is able to generate 10 percent on its assets but is able to borrow money at 5 percent. To start, the company has, say, $1 million of assets. If it has no liabilities, its return on assets and return on equity are both 10 percent ($1,000,000 of assets times a 10 percent return yields $100,000). Its equity is also $1 million, as there are no liabilities to subtract.

Now, let's look at a scenario where the business borrows $9 million at 5 percent (yes, it was possible to do so, for the reasons described above) to buy $9 million of additional assets that yield 10 percent. At least for the short run, the company is doing great. The company now has $10 million of assets ($1,000,000 original plus $9,000,000 purchased with borrowed money) and still has $1 million of equity ($10,000,000 of assets less $9,000,000 of liabilities). The $10 million of assets yield 10 percent, or $1 million. The $9 million of liabilities cost $450,000 annually ($9,000,000 times a 5 percent cost of capital, or interest expense), leaving $550,000 of return ($1,000,000 of yield on the asset base less the $450,000 of interest expense). While the return on assets remains fixed at 10 percent, the return on equity has now jumped from 10 percent to 55 percent ($550,000 divided by $1,000,000 of equity)!

Things on Wall Street were terrific—bonuses were rich, and the investment banks seemed invincible. Oh yeah, until the write-downs. Taking a mere 10 percent loss on the $10 million of assets in this example now values the assets at $9 million. With $9 million of liabilities, the stockholders' equity has now been completely wiped out. Imagine the pain with similar (or worse) asset value declines when the leverage employed was not a 10 times debt-to-equity ratio but a 40 times debt-to-equity ratio!

Uncle Sam stepped in in a big way, offering more cheap financing to the institutions it deemed "too big to fail." It set up (at least) a program to buy from these companies what were now called "toxic assets," generally referring to the loan pools. AIG was extended $182.5 billion dollars in credit in exchange for a 79.9 percent warrant to purchase AIG shares. Banks were forced to accept equity capital from the U.S. government, leaving taxpayers as large owners of the financial system. The process ultimately stabilized the country, but partial nationalization of the industry was required. What the government does with its newfound influence on these firms has yet to be fully seen.

In addition to pumping hundreds of billions of dollars of equity capital into banks and other financial concerns, the U.S. government ensured the repayment of loans issued by these institutions under an emergency guarantee program. Banks get money by accepting deposits into checking and savings accounts as well as certificates of deposit (CDs) and borrowing money at low interest rates. They take those funds and loan the money to businesses and homeowners at higher rates. The difference, the interest rate spread, is critical. That spread, multiplied by the assets under management, is the primary source of their operating funds.

When confidence of repayment waned during the financial crisis, the taxpayer backing allowed potentially weak borrowers to secure funding at artificially low rates through the Temporary Liquidity Guarantee Program. This cheap money pumped up short-term profitability as it widened the interest rate spread and helped offset the heightened impairment of their asset bases as many loans were written down or written off due to defaults. Again, the taxpayers took the risk but the federal guarantees were not reflected in the U.S. government's balance sheet as contingent liabilities. Once the program ends, the banks will be required to resort to market-based interest rates, and their cost of capital will depend on how fiscally sound they are perceived to be. For example, Citibank recently issued $2 billion of nonguaranteed bonds due in 2014 with a 5.5 percent interest rate. JPMorgan Chase, on the other hand, was able to borrow $1.5 billion due in 2015 with a mere 3.7 percent coupon. The interest rates will be able to charge for loans they make to individuals and businesses will be similar and determined by competitive forces. So JPMorgan's future profitability looks much brighter due to almost 2 additional percentage points of interest rate spread because of its perceived stronger financial position.

In September 2009, the Federal Housing Administration (FHA), which insures lenders against losses on home mortgages, decided to tighten credit requirements on the loans it guarantees. In line with government-backed mortgage investors Fannie Mae and Freddie Mac, the FHA will now impose a maximum loan-to-value ratio on refinanced mortgages of 125 percent of the home's value. In other words, they'll extend you a $125,000 mortgage on a $100,000 house, $25,000 (20 percent) of which is immediately unsecured (more when foreclosure and sale expenses are deducted from any ultimate recovery). On new purchases, the FHA requires only a 3.5 percent down payment. As you might imagine, demand for such financing has increased substantially, growing from about 2 percent of new home mortgages in 2006 to nearly 25 percent in the third quarter of 2009. It should come as no surprise that about 14 percent of mortgages the Federal Housing Administration guarantees were 30 days or more past due or in foreclosure as of September 2009.

Of course, homeowners who become delinquent on these loans generally don't keep up with requisite repairs and improvements, so the likely collateral value to support the FHA guarantees upon foreclosure and subsequent sale will deteriorate further. Incredibly, the agency has stated that its supplementary reserves for the loans it insures will fall below the 2 percent legal minimum. The agency employs leverage of 50:1! Bear Stearns, just prior to its collapse in 2008, had a debt-to-equity ratio of a measly 33:1. Talk about hypocrisy.

It would seem logical to dramatically increase underwriting standards. A 20 percent down payment, for example, would provide a reasonable cushion against default, covering foreclosure and sale costs and some potential value deterioration. Similarly, a refinancing limit of 80 percent of a home's appraised worth would protect the FHA from future losses. Having more "skin in the game" also provides incentive for homeowners to find a way to keep current on their mortgages instead of handing over the keys to the bank when real estate prices fall and their property's value declines below the amount they owe.

The problem that imposing reason into this process creates, however, is that many people will be shut out of the home-buying process. There are those in government who have attempted to make home ownership a right, not a privilege, regardless of creditworthiness. The Federal Housing Enterprises Financial Safety and Soundness Act of 1992 required Fannie Mae and Freddie Mac to devote a percentage of their lending to support affordable housing. Government guarantees by the FHA and mortgage purchases by Freddie Mac and Fannie Mae have brought many fringe buyers into the game. Real estate values jumped in the first decade of the new millennium due to the large number of incremental buyers able to qualify for mortgages. If lending standards were tightened to more reasonable levels, these extra buyers would now be out of the game. With fewer bidders for the available home supply, house prices would decline further. Said additional decrease would result in bigger losses for the more than $6 *trillion* in real estate loans the U.S. government owns or guarantees. So Uncle Sam can't politically or economically afford not to continue to artificially prop up property values. This is evidenced by a *Wall Street Journal* report in September 2009 that the Obama administration was launching an initiative to commit an additional $35 billion to "help beleaguered state and local housing agencies to provide mortgages to low- and moderate-income families."[1] Taxpayers now guarantee repayment on more than 80 percent of all U.S. mortgages! What a mess.

RATING AGENCIES

There are concerns that provide "independent" assessments of other companies' business prospects, along with their balance sheet strength, in order to assess their creditworthiness for lenders. Such companies include Standard & Poor's Corp., Moody's Investor Service Inc., and Fitch Ratings Inc. These three in particular maintain a privileged status with the U.S. government as Nationally Recognized Statistical Rating Organizations (NRSROs). Primarily used by prospective lenders to consider making credit available to businesses seeking financing, these entities will evaluate the borrower's historical and anticipated future profitability, current debt levels, customer concentration, and other determining factors—for a fee. The problem with this structure is that the entity that ultimately pays the fees to the rating agencies is the one being rated. In other words, the rating agencies have an inherent conflict of interest in providing favorable ratings in order to secure current and future business. The three companies use slightly different grading. A general long-term issuer credit rating overview (used by Standard and Poor's Corp., also known as S&P) follows as described on its Web site:

AAA: An obligor rated AAA has extremely strong capacity to meet its financial commitments. AAA is the highest issuer credit rating assigned by Standard & Poor's. The U.S. government maintains a triple A rating on its debt (as of this writing).

AA: An obligor rated AA has very strong capacity to meet its financial commitments. It differs from the highest-rated obligors only to a small degree.

A: An obligor rated A has strong capacity to meet its financial commitments but is somewhat more susceptible to the adverse effects of changes in circumstances and economic conditions than obligors in higher-rated categories.

BBB: An obligor rated BBB has adequate capacity to meet its financial commitments. However, adverse economic conditions or changing circumstances are more likely to lead to a weakened capacity of the obligor to meet its financial commitments.

BB, B, CCC, and CC: Obligors rated BB, B, CCC, and CC are regarded
as having significant speculative characteristics. BB indicates the
least degree of speculation, and CC the highest. While such
obligors will likely have some quality and protective
characteristics, these may be outweighed by large uncertainties
or major exposures to adverse conditions.

An obligor rated BB is less vulnerable in the near term than other
lower-rated obligors. However, it faces major ongoing
uncertainties and exposure to adverse business, financial, or
economic conditions, which could lead to the obligor's inadequate
capacity to meet its financial commitments.

An obligor rated B is more vulnerable than the obligors rated BB,
but the obligor currently has the capacity to meet its financial
commitments. Adverse business, financial, or economic
conditions will likely impair the obligor's capacity or willingness
to meet its financial commitments.

An obligor rated CCC is currently vulnerable, and is dependent
upon favorable business, financial, and economic conditions to
meet its financial commitments.

An obligor rated CC is currently highly vulnerable.

An obligor rated R is under regulatory supervision owing to its
financial condition. During the pendency of the regulatory
supervision, the regulators may have the power to favor one class
of obligations over others or pay some obligations and not others.

An obligor rated SD (selective default) or D has failed to pay
one or more of its financial obligations (rated or unrated) when
they came due. A D rating is assigned when Standard & Poor's
believes that the default will be a general default and that the

obligor will fail to pay all or substantially all of its obligations as they come due.

An SD rating is assigned when Standard & Poor's believes that the obligor has selectively defaulted on a specific issue or class of obligations but that it will continue to meet its payment obligations on other issues or classes of obligations in a timely manner.

A selective default includes the completion of a distressed exchange offer, whereby one or more financial obligations are either repurchased for an amount of cash or replaced by other instruments having a total value that is less than par.

A Standard & Poor's issue credit rating is a current opinion of the creditworthiness of an obligor with respect to a specific financial obligation, a specific class of financial obligations, or a specific financial program (including ratings on medium-term note programs and commercial paper programs). It takes into consideration the creditworthiness of guarantors, insurers, or other forms of credit enhancement on the obligation and takes into account the currency in which the obligation is denominated. The opinion evaluates the obligor's capacity and willingness to meet its financial commitments as they come due, and may assess terms, such as collateral security and subordination, which could affect ultimate payment in the event of default. Issue credit ratings can be either long term or short term. Short-term ratings are generally assigned to those obligations with an original maturity of no more than 365 days, including commercial paper.

Table 8.1 on page 128 lists the percentage of defaults of obligors that had been assigned various S&P debt ratings. As you can see, the higher the rating, the lower the chance of default.

Just like an individual seeking a mortgage, the higher a company's credit rating, the lower the interest expense it will have to bear. Many

Table 8.1 Standard & Poor's One-Year Global Corporate Default Rates by Refined Rating Category

	AAA	AA+	AA	AA-	A	A+	A-	BBB+	BBB	BBB-	BB+	BB	BB-	B+	B	B-	CCC to C
1994	–	–	–	–	0.45	–	–	–	–	–	–	0.86	–	1.83	6.58	3.23	16.67
1995	–	–	–	–	–	–	–	–	–	0.63	–	1.55	1.11	2.76	8.00	7.69	28.00
1996	–	–	–	–	–	–	–	–	–	–	0.86	0.65	0.55	2.33	3.74	3.92	4.17
1997	–	–	–	–	–	–	–	0.36	0.34	–	–	–	0.41	0.72	5.19	14.58	12.00
1998	–	–	–	–	–	–	–	–	0.54	0.70	1.29	1.06	0.72	2.57	7.47	9.46	42.86
1999	–	–	–	0.36	–	0.24	0.27	–	0.28	0.30	0.54	1.33	0.90	4.20	10.55	15.45	32.35
2000	–	–	–	–	–	0.24	0.56	–	0.26	0.88	–	0.80	2.29	5.60	10.66	11.50	34.12
2001	–	–	–	–	0.57	0.49	–	0.24	0.48	0.27	0.49	1.19	6.27	5.94	15.74	23.31	44.55
2002	–	–	–	–	–	–	–	1.11	0.65	1.31	1.50	1.74	4.62	3.69	9.63	19.53	44.12
2003	–	–	–	–	–	–	–	–	0.19	0.52	0.48	0.94	0.27	1.70	5.16	9.23	33.13
2004	–	–	–	–	–	0.23	–	–	–	–	–	0.64	0.76	0.46	2.68	2.82	15.11
2005	–	–	–	–	–	–	–	–	0.17	–	0.36	–	0.25	0.78	2.59	2.98	8.87
2006	–	–	–	–	–	–	–	–	–	–	0.36	–	0.48	0.54	0.78	1.58	13.08
2007	–	–	–	–	–	–	–	–	–	–	–	0.30	0.23	0.19	–	0.88	14.81
2008	–	–	0.43	0.40	0.31	0.21	0.58	0.18	0.59	0.71	1.14	0.63	0.63	2.97	3.29	7.02	26.53
Mean	–	–	0.02	0.03	0.05	0.06	0.08	0.16	0.28	0.28	0.68	0.89	1.53	2.44	7.28	9.97	22.67

lenders rely on these ratings when making decisions about how much to lend to a given borrower, what rate to charge, and how quickly repayment will be required.

Perhaps due the complexity of some of the obligations that have been rated or the inherent conflict of interest that rating agencies have, major problems have resulted from inaccurate grading of debt instruments. The overly generous evaluations granted to many of the structured investment vehicles referred to previously allowed their owners to borrow money in tranches against them. These tranches were essentially first, second, and third mortgages secured by the SIVs. Because the rating agencies gave the tranches high marks (with the first tranche obviously getting the highest grade of the three), billions of dollars were lent using the SIVs as collateral. The rating agencies did not anticipate the dramatic real estate value declines that were forthcoming. Consequently, the delinquencies, foreclosures, and haircuts to the SIV values resulted in unprecedented losses to investors.

In July 2009, the nation's largest pension fund, the California Public Employees' Retirement System, or CalPERS, filed a lawsuit in California state court in conjunction with $1 billion in losses that CalPERS claims were caused by misleading credit ratings from the three leading ratings agencies. CalPERS contends that, in giving these packages of securities the agencies' highest credit rating, Moody's, Standard & Poor's, and Fitch "made negligent misrepresentations" to the pension fund. CalPERS manages retirement assets for nearly two million public employees in California.

The AAA ratings provided to the SIVs by the agencies "proved to be wildly inaccurate and unreasonably high" according the lawsuit; it also contended that the methodologies utilized to assess these collateral packages "were seriously flawed in conception and incompetently applied." In the case of the SIVs that are subject to this dispute, the three rating agencies allegedly received substantial fees not only for rating the asset pools' creditworthiness *but also for helping to structure the deals themselves*.

The lawsuit also argues that the rating agencies continued to publicly promote structured investment vehicles even while beginning to downgrade them. Ten days after Moody's had downgraded some securitized packages in 2007, it issued a report titled "Structured Investment Vehicles: An Oasis of Calm in the Subprime Maelstrom."

In an effort to help stabilize the financial system in late 2008 and early 2009, the U.S. government provided inexpensive loans to banks and other lenders. These loans required collateral (often other loans to entities holding pools of mortgages) having AAA ratings. The Fed has taken significant losses on these extensions of credit due to the insufficiency of the collateral provided, despite the high ratings.

Ratings agencies have also come under fire for the sovereign debt ratings that have been issued to various countries worldwide. Almost all nations issue debt. The ratings issued on these obligations have a major impact on each country's interest expense. An unfavorable rating may cost taxpayers many billions of dollars (or local currency equivalent) annually. Given that S&P, Moody's, and Fitch seek to provide their services within each worldwide jurisdiction, certain implicit or explicit pressure may be applied by countries to secure the most favorable ratings possible. This winds up hurting those investors that rely on such ratings (probably too much so) in making financial decisions.

Many contend that the rating agencies have an inherent conflict of interest and are notoriously slow in recognizing corporate improvement or decline. Often, upon a company releasing annual financial statements and a corresponding outlook, the agencies' view changes. In other words, they are reactionary. Once a company reports poor earnings, it may then be downgraded to a lower rating tier. But by then it is generally too late for the investor to react, because the price of the debt and equity in the company have already declined. This is, to some degree, a result of the relatively inferior wages offered by the rating agencies to their analysts. Wall Street securities firms generally pay much more.

Insurance companies often use the monies they receive from premiums to purchase bonds (and other assets) in order to generate income on investment portfolios. They collectively hold roughly $3 trillion in rated bonds as investments. The ratings agencies are under attack here as well. State insurance regulators have been reported to be considering moving away from utilizing grades from Standard & Poor's and Moody's when evaluating the value of the assets the insurance companies list on their balance sheets. This is important because insurance companies are required to maintain sufficient reserves to pay policyholders' claims when they come due. A hit to assets is directly subtracted from equity, as liabilities remain unchanged when asset levels change. The change in regulators' perspective stems in part to the rapid decline in the ratings provided for residential mortgage-backed securities from 2005 to 2007. In fact, of those securities that were rated triple A in 2005, less than one-third maintained the AAA label by 2007. More than 40 percent of the previously deemed AAA securities were downgraded to C or D ratings during this time.

As discussed, throughout the financial crisis, the credit ratings institutions were often criticized for overly rosy ratings of complex debt securities. Such obligations subsequently deteriorated in value and led to billions of dollars of investor losses. An analyst for Moody's in September 2009 brought concerns to the U.S. Congress that the firm knowingly issued and continued to issue inflated ratings, stating that those responsible for ensuring sound ratings methodology are "routinely bullied" by management. A congressional committee has called on Moody's Corp. to respond to the allegations that its Moody's Investors Service unit continues to inflate credit ratings, largely due to conflicts of interest arising from the fact that the firm is paid by debt issuers to rate securities.

One primary charge is that Moody's allegedly gave a high rating to complicated debt securities in January 2009 while knowing that it was planning to downgrade assets that backed the securities. Within months, the securities in question were put on review for downgrade. Following the hearing of the National Association of Insurance Commissioners in September 2009, Wisconsin's insurance commissioner stated, "It's clear to me we can no longer rely solely on the ratings agencies" when determining the fiscal strength of insurance companies.

One company that compiles payment histories for many small, private businesses is Dun & Bradstreet (D&B). Dun & Bradstreet gets records of late payments from vendors, lawsuit filing data, and credit reports from financial institutions on companies as small as the local drycleaner. This information is invaluable to companies considering extending payment terms to a small customer. The cost of such investigations is worth it, as it could save a company many thousands of dollars in bad debt expense write-offs.

Wall Street

How much things have changed yet remain the same. Wall Street titans like Merrill Lynch, Bear Stearns, and Lehman Brothers crumbled in the late 2000s. Yet the fact remains that corporations are dependent on the services that Wall Street still provides. These services include introductions to or advice about mergers and acquisitions, investment management, risk management tools (including commodity and currency fluctuation hedging as well as customer debt default protection), and of course, finding money.

Companies that seek to raise debt or equity capital via the corporate finance divisions of investment banks often need to pay eye-popping fees to get the funding they seek. For without the extra money, growth options are often limited to those available using internally generated cash flow. In conjunction with the capital raises, the investment banks are often utilized to assign research analysts to "cover the company." In doing so, the generally positive research reports highlight the corporate finance customer's merits and downplay any negative developments. Just like auditing concerns that get consulting fees or rating agencies that get paid to issue debt gradings, the investment banks have a built-in conflict of interest. There is supposed to be a "Chinese Wall" between the investment banking and research departments within these organizations, but the reality is that the barbarians almost invariably find a way to breach the divide.

You may wonder whom you can trust. The short answer is: no one but yourself. If insufficient information is provided in a company's financial statements and related notes, don't invest. Lack of transparency is a huge red flag. Also, examine the financial statements for the issues I've addressed here. While mistakes are still likely, they'll be drastically reduced. Also, there is no substitute for hard work. Calling the vendors of a business to question their payment experience may be a great way to find out a company's true fiscal strength. Remember that vendor payment stretching is often a first sign of trouble. Consider how well a business is faring relative to its competition: Is growth comparable? Is it losing market share? Try out its products or services as a prospective customer; determine for yourself the strength of the company's value proposition, for customers ultimately determine its success or failure. Don't be afraid to peel the proverbial onion.

Now that we've looked at some public and private problems recently encountered, let's look at how decision makers may prudently manage the balance sheet resources at their disposal.

9

EFFECTIVE BALANCE SHEET MANAGEMENT TECHNIQUES

MANAGING RISK AND PROTECTING ASSETS

"I'm frightened!" you may be thinking. "If there are so many potential pitfalls, how do I avoid stepping into a bear trap?" First of all, you'll never completely avoid risk (other than through the purchase of assets like inflation-indexed U.S. Treasury bonds, which pay you very little but provide extra money if the dollar weakens in value). From a corporate perspective, use common sense. Some key areas to focus on for safety follow.

Minimizing Debt

Companies that use little leverage are less likely to default on their obligations. This conservative approach may slow a company's growth because fewer cash resources will be available to management for investments in equipment, advertising, corporate acquisitions, bulk inventory, and other revenue and profit-enhancing opportunities. On the other hand, the potentially wild swings that can come with heavy debt loads will be avoided, and you'll sleep better.

The higher the level of liabilities, the greater the portion of operating profit that needs to be utilized to amortize the debt and pay interest expense. In addition, firms that carry large debt loads relative to their ability to generate cash flow generally bear a higher cost of capital. In other words, the interest rate on any new borrowings goes up considerably to compensate any lender for taking a higher risk on the investment. These are funds that could otherwise be used to purchase new equipment or finance growth opportunities. This potential lack of future reinvestment can make a business less competitive in the longer term, further increasing the risk of default.

If a company fails to pay its liabilities as they come due and can't secure additional loans to refinance the debt, additional funds pro rata from existing shareholders may be needed (a *rights offering*), new equity capital may be sought from new shareholders (diluting the ownership percentage of the original owners), or a bankruptcy filing may ensue. The bankruptcy filing may wipe out any value to shareholders or cause the defaulted debt to be converted into substantial ownership of the company, providing substantial dilution. The benefit of this restructuring process is that the company's balance sheet becomes much more deleveraged. With a lower debt load subsequent to the balance sheet reorganization, much more of the company's future cash flow may be used to grow the business. You don't want to pay that price, if possible. Avoiding the excessive debt in the first place achieves that goal.

Finding Strong Management

At the end of the day, it is more important to have great people than a great business plan. Smart managers will steer a ship through stormy waters. Look for managers who have a long, ethical track record. Having an incentive plan that rewards employees without the temptation to cook the books is important. Remember that it is easy to fool auditors. Seasoned professionals with clean backgrounds are worth their weight in gold. Who do you want to manage your assets?

Diversifying

Make sure that you own a basket of stocks with no single investment composing a substantial percentage of your net worth. The shares should be held in a variety of industries in a variety of countries. The portion of your portfolio invested in stocks should in turn be balanced with commodities and debt obligations, each of which should be spread out. The best way to do so is through index funds, which are cheap to own and provide great diversification.

From an individual business evaluation perspective, make sure that a company's customer base is diversified. You don't want to run the risk that a business loses its only buyer of goods or services. It is also important that a company has multiple vendor options so that it may switch suppliers should one raise prices or discontinue operations. The automakers, for example, are very dependent on certain suppliers. General Motors has essentially agreed to reacquire Delphi, a major parts supplier, in part to protect the flow of parts to its factories. In

October 2009, Chrysler had to shut down production of several Jeep models due to "stress in the automotive supply chain."

Seeking Long-Term Contracts

Companies that operate on a one-off, month-to-month basis with the constant stress of replacing individual sales are risky bets. Look at the example of a lawn cutting business that has 100 accounts, including contracts with homeowner associations. Every week, the business mows the lawns and is generally paid on time. The customer base is solid and enjoys very little customer concentration while benefiting from long-term maintenance contracts. Another landscaping company might do only landscape design and installation. The design and installation business may have higher gross margins, but once the work is performed the next job must be sought. An economic downturn could have devastating effects on the design-and-install company while the maintenance business flows right along.

Maintaining Insurance

One way for a business to go south in a hurry is to lack sufficient insurance protection. Some obvious types of insurance that must be carried protect real estate from fire, water, or other damage. Under a general liability insurance policy, the insurer is obligated to pay the legal costs of a business in a covered liability claim or lawsuit. Covered general liability claims include bodily injury, property damage, personal injury, and advertising injury (damage from slander or false advertising).

Worker's compensation is a form of insurance that provides compensation medical care for employees who are injured in the course of employment, in exchange for mandatory relinquishment of the employee's right to sue his or her employer for the tort of negligence. Automobile (or truck) insurance pays to fix vehicle repairs from an accident as well any medical bills from injuries or claims from litigation resulting from damage to property or people. A service business might seek errors and omissions (E&O) insurance, which protects the company from accidental oversights that might cause harm. An example might be an accounting firm that made a mistake in the preparation of financial statements. Investors purchasing securities based on the information in the faulty financial statements that lost money may have recourse to recuperate losses with the E&O policy.

Malpractice insurance is critical for doctors and other licensed professionals to cover litigation expenses and payments resulting from actual or alleged treatment errors. If one or a few executives are critical to the operation of the business, key man life insurance may be purchased. To the extent that an important manager passes away, the company will receive sufficient funds to find new talent and pay investors. Business interruption insurance, as the name implies, pays a company for unexpected downtime due to a number of factors, including weather or fire.

Default protection may be purchased for key customers; if they don't pay their bills, the guarantor will step in and make you whole. Internet business insurance covers liability for damage done by hackers and viruses. In addition, e-insurance often covers specialized online activities, including lawsuits resulting from mega tag abuse, banner advertising, or electronic copyright infringement. Criminal insurance protects firms from risks such as computer hacking, vandalism, general theft, or employee embezzlement. Product liability insurance defends against claims related to a sold product's safety—businesses may be considered liable for negligence, breach of an express or implied warranty, defective products, and/or defective warnings or instructions.

An umbrella insurance policy adds additional liability protection above and beyond any of the individual policies. There is even executive kidnapping coverage to pay a ransom should the need arise. With the abundance of lawyers looking for contingency fees and no tort reform likely any time soon, consider insurance premiums to be a necessary cost of doing business. Obviously, the perceived risks of a potential claim must be measured against the premium expense.

From an individual's perspective, assets may be protected with insurance just as with a business. Homeowner's insurance, auto insurance, life insurance, health insurance, and an umbrella policy are all prudent uses of resources. Disability insurance, which pays you if you're unable to work, is exceptionally expensive, though. If you're able to get by without direct access to some assets, make regular contributions into vehicles that are protected from creditors.

Retirement plans such as 401(k)s or individual retirement accounts (IRAs), are protected from litigation and other claims. Other attractive options to protect assets include investing in medical savings accounts or educational savings plans for children or grandchildren. Another means by which you may shelter assets from fallout is to create a trust for the benefit of others, often kids. Trusts provide strong asset protection but require the loss of control of the funds contributed. Trust income is also taxed at high rates.

As discussed at the outset, the two primary financial statements that describe an organization's fiscal well-being are the income statement and balance sheet. I have intentionally omitted the third leg of the stool, the cash flow statement. This has been done because the cash flow statement is purely illustrative in nature. Nevertheless, it is worth a short overview.

CHAPTER

10

THE CASH FLOW STATEMENT

WHY THE CASH FLOW STATEMENT IS NOT IMPORTANT

There are many folks out there who would have you believe that there are three main financial statements: the income statement (P&L), the balance sheet, and the cash flow statement. As discussed, the income statement shows how much money is made or lost over a period of time, and the balance sheet shows what is owned, owed, and left over at a specific point in time. Both provide hugely valuable information. *Assuming that the balance sheets provide sufficient detail*, the cash flow statement, however, provides no new significant information.

The cash flow statement is actually quite simple. It starts with net income (or loss), copied from the income statement. Then it shows the increase or decrease in the level of assets and liabilities on the balance sheet over a specified time (the same time period used for the corresponding income statement). The cash flow statement adds net income to the increase or decrease in cash resulting from the balance sheet changes, leaving you with total change in cash. Start with beginning cash amount, add or subtract the change in cash over the specified time period, and get the ending cash amount. The cash flow statement's entries come from the other two statements; provided that the balance sheets have sufficient detail, it provides no new information.

Don't get me wrong, the cash flow statement may make it easier for you to see how much more you've borrowed (by subtracting ending debt from beginning debt) or how much more your customers owe you in the form of accounts receivable (again, by subtracting the ending receivables balance from the beginning receivables balance). But the information is merely illustrative; it does not provide anything new. The four components of the cash flow statement are net income, operating activities, investing activities, and financing activities.

Net Income

The *net income* is simply copied from the income statement for the same time period. We'll call net income "W."

Operating Activities

Those things that impact changes in current assets and current liabilities are *operating activities*. How much have accounts payable gone up? This would be a source of cash in excess of net income, as net income is already "depressed" by the expense even though it has not been paid. How much has inventory increased? This would be a use of cash because the purchase of extra inventory would not be reflected in net income but would reduce cash through the asset transfer from cash to inventory. How much have prepaid expenses, or deposits, increased? This would be a use of cash, as the extra deposits take cash without the corresponding expense.

Succinctly, when current assets go up, cash is used, or transferred, into other short-term asset forms. Conversely, when current liabilities go up, cash is sourced through the increase of short-term types of liabilities; you're effectively borrowing extra money, often from payroll taxes payable, accrued expenses, or trade accounts payable.

These figures may be easily calculated by subtracting the beginning-of-period assets or liabilities from the end-of-period assets or liabilities. If end-of-period short-term assets are higher than beginning-of-period current assets, the difference is a use of cash (and vice versa). If end-of-period short term liabilities are higher than beginning-of-period current liabilities, the difference is a source of cash (and vice versa).

Adding the net increase (or decrease) in current assets to that of current liabilities yields *total operating activities*. We'll label total operating activities "X."

Investing Activities

When you buy a new item—say, a backhoe—you must pay money for the long-term asset but you won't have recorded an expense immediately. This transfer of money from cash to equipment reduces cash and is not recorded in net income, as the equipment is not expensed immediately because the value is not immediately lost. Because the long-term assets are generally used to operate the business, it is said that an investment is made into the company. When long-term assets are purchased, cash is used as an *investing activity*. When long-term assets are sold, cash is generated.

Depreciation and amortization are expenses on the income statement that depress net income but don't require cash outlays during the specified period. In fact, depreciation and amortization basically just represent the decline in value of the tangible assets being depreciated or intangible assets being amortized. These are balance sheet long-term asset changes that are also considered investing activities. The decline in asset values from depreciation and amortization reflects a source of cash, as the correlated expense is noncash in nature.

Again, these figures are net balance sheet value changes. We'll call total investing activities "Y."

Financing Activities

Borrowing or repaying long-term debt and receiving or paying back equity investments are *financing activities*. Borrowing money provides cash without impacting the income statement. (It would be silly to consider the new cash to be revenue.) Repaying money uses cash without impacting the income statement; labeling such repayment an expense would be inappropriate.

Long-term debt, as previously discussed, may come in the form of bank loans, borrowings from bondholders, equipment loans, or real estate mortgages. The increase or decrease in these long-term obligations is a major component of financing activities on the cash flow statement.

The other piece of the financing activities part of the cash flow statement is *equity capital*. Equity capital changes are composed of increases in paid-in capital (through additional cash investment) or decreases in paid-in capital resulting from buying out an owner's stake or dividends (pro-rata payout to shareholders). Paid-in capital may include both common and preferred stock.

The net change in all equity and debt on the balance sheet for the stipulated time period is *total financing activities*. We'll call total financing activities "Z."

Total Change in Cash

Let's start with the beginning balance sheet's cash balance. From there, we add or subtract the four ways the cash balance may be modified, yielding the ending cash balance.

In short, beginning cash balance plus net income plus total operating activities plus total investing activities plus total financing activities equals ending cash balance:

$$\text{Beginning Cash} + W + X + Y + Z = \text{Ending Cash}$$

The cash balance listed on a year-end statement is the beginning cash balance to start the next year. Over the following 12 months, assets and liabilities will go up or down. The net result of the asset and liability changes, coupled with any income or loss, will determine the following year's ending cash balance.

Note that total operating activities, total investing activities, and total financing activities may each be negative if they use more cash than they provide. Net income may be a net loss if expenses exceed revenue. Even cash may be negative if checks are written for which insufficient cash exists in the corresponding checking account.

11

COMMON MISTAKES WHEN STARTING A BUSINESS

Many people who venture out on their own don't anticipate some problems they encounter due to a lack of understanding of financial statements or similar challenges. Many cooks and bartenders, for example, see the owner "pocket" what seems to be a huge amount of money in a short time. The illusion that this received revenue somehow equates to profit has led to an overabundance of restaurants, most of which ultimately fail.

The biggest initial problem faced by new entrepreneurs is lack of funding. Because few see every expense absorbed by their former employer, not all costs are anticipated. In the case of a restaurant, much of the food is thrown out; facility rental may be expensive; accountant fees can be high; air conditioning, heat, and other utilities are costly; employees and payroll taxes are onerous; upgrading equipment, seating, and fixtures is necessary on a regular basis; and advertising expenditures may be prohibitive but necessary to fill the seats. Consequently, the income statement projections used to justify the initial decision are often overly optimistic. Six months after the formation of the company (and the initial euphoria), the business is nearly out of money and the owner is working 90 hours per week because payroll is too high.

A smart way to start a new business is to prepare while you are still on someone else's payroll. Evaluate the need for the product or service you are considering offering. Try to line up customers, if possible. This might be done for a consulting gig more easily than a car wash, for example. Of course, such customer presolicitation might run afoul of your current employer's loyalty and expectations. A friend of mine at Price Waterhouse (PW) built a lucrative consulting practice by offering his services directly to PW clients at a lower billing rate than that charged by the big six (at the time, anyway) accounting firm. He succeeded, and dramatically increased his current income, but caused his former employer's resentment. His strategy might have backfired, however, if the clients had refused his advance and informed his bosses. Be careful!

Projected financial statement preparation is essential, both for planning purposes as well as to share with prospective financial partners or lenders. It is critical to include both an income statement and balance sheet. The income statement determines when you expect to become profitable; the balance sheet, more importantly, reflects how much *cash* you'll have at any given point. Create monthly projections using conservative assumptions. Look at the annual reports of public companies in similar industries, and mimic their expense categories. You don't want to jump in with both feet if you've neglected to plan for marketing cash needs.

Get actual insurance premium quotes, rental costs and deposit requirements, labor and advertising rates, and utility costs. Take out as much risk as possible. Plan on slow revenue growth. Build in an expense cushion. Expect only a small income for yourself for many, many hours of work. If the numbers don't work on that basis and your cash balance is likely to near zero, don't proceed! Of course, you'll make mistakes along the way, but don't ever let emotion get in the way of rational decision making. Just because you like to bake doesn't mean that opening a bakery down the street is an intelligent decision. If you need help, drop me a note at Rick@InAnHour.com.

Other means of preparation that may be accomplished safely (prior to jumping ship) include research on locations (for retail establishments) or overall demand in the area for your intended offerings. How many similar establishments are already there? How are they doing? Are pricing pressures too great? Is there adequate parking? I once opened a coffee shop in a location that lacked a parking lot. Foot traffic alone was insufficient to generate a worthwhile profit. Luckily, I was able to sell the building (which also benefitted from other rental revenue) at a premium.

Having tangible assets, most notably real estate, will make the business funding much more easily attainable. Unless you are sitting on a big pile of cash or have rich relatives, you will almost definitely need personal credit to get started. Plan to write a big check and to guarantee a bank loan. Access to such a loan is facilitated with real estate as collateral. The property may be your primary residence or the building in which the business will reside.

Another important consideration is the form of the corporate structure you'll use. Many people nowadays use limited liability companies due to the legal protections they provide as well as the avoidance of double taxation. Keep in mind that you need at least two members (owners) in an LLC to be taxed like a partnership. Consult your legal advisor, as regulations and protections vary by state.

Learn from others. If you're considering opening (or buying, for that matter) a company, look at the annual reports of similar businesses for gross margins, revenue trends, expense categories, and pitfalls. Business lines that offer franchises (ranging from car repair to sandwich makers) have franchisors that provide instruction manuals derived over time from the lessons learned by others. Benefit from their pain. It is much easier to read about how to succeed than to take your lumps trying to get there the hard way. Remember McDowell's restaurant in *Coming To America* (with Eddie Murphy)? Very funny flick, if you haven't seen it.

Make sure to keep accurate records. Plan to pay a bookkeeper on a monthly basis to update your financial records in an accounting software package such as QuickBooks or Peachtree. These tools also allow you to write checks and record expenses. If you stay on top of this process, it will be easy to print out an income statement or balance sheet whenever needed. Importantly, tax preparation will be facilitated for your accountant, saving him or her time, and you, money. If done correctly, the analysis of the numbers in your accounting system will help you fine-tune business strategy. You may find that the sale of certain products is considerably more (gross) profitable than the sale of others. Such revelations may result in a positive change in marketing focus or a discontinuation of unprofitable pursuits.

USE THIS BOOK TO IMPROVE MANAGEMENT SKILLS

Whether you oversee a large corporation or a small group, your goals need to be clear. A plan to execute business objectives needs to be constructed and continually refined as circumstances and priorities change. One general mantra permeates all specific plans: *Maximize shareholder value*. Let me be clear—you work to make money for the owner or owners of the business. All decisions should be prioritized accordingly. A salesperson who accepts an unprofitable contract to get a commission is acting on his or her own behalf while hurting the employer. If the ship that supports its people sinks, all on board drown. Every employee needs to operate with this slogan in mind. Each division must be viewed as an independent profit center. Growing profitable sales and mitigating costs is the backbone of any business strategy. If your specific group does not directly solicit revenue from customers, such as a human resources department, keep costs way, way down. Logical employers will recognize the value contribution and will reward those that pull for the team appropriately.

Being Organized

Good organization is essential. Starting with your ultimate goal of maximizing value to the company's owners, make a list of the tasks needed to do so. Then rank the responsibilities in order of priority. This task may seem simple, but sometimes putting the list on paper will reduce anxiety and provide comfortable assurance that the necessary steps are being completed. Keep records of the chores as they are done as well as the time required for each task. In this manner, you will be able to gauge how much time should be allocated for similar jobs going forward. Have a weekly meeting to assess progress, add new assignments, and continually evaluate the relative priorities of each undertaking.

Using Tools

Technology is our friend. Having a computer system that handles scheduling, for example, may reduce the need for administrative assistants. A giant shredder that cuts up steel at a scrap yard may save the expense of 10 employees along with their torches and fuel. Cheap teleconferencing saves money otherwise spent on travel as well as the associated wasted time. Encourage employees in the weekly meeting to offer suggestions as to how and what tools may help the business.

Communicating

Communication is key. It is important that people within each division talk about their successes and challenges. In this fashion, everyone will learn and grow to be more effective over time. Division heads should also meet regularly in order to avoid effort duplication and to take advantage of cost consolidation or cross-selling opportunities.

Operating Efficiently

If employee compensation is fixed, get as many hours of work from those salaried employees as possible. Lead by example. Yes, people want free time to spend with families and friends. In the bigger picture, though, job security is paramount. One's income provides food and shelter for spouses and children. The best way to protect them is to maximize profits for one's employer. Once the business thrives, due at least in part to the hardworking staff, discretionary bonuses will keep valuable people loyal. These "extra" chunks of cash can be viewed as long-term security as we prepare a nest egg for eventual retirement. On the other hand, those employees who lag should be targets for elimination. No one should consider his or her employment a right. Sometimes the firing of one or two slackers will provide incentive to the rest to work harder and stay later.

Other sources of efficiency come from the tools mentioned above or from management's direction of employee decisions. Achieving extra productivity from equipment or people is a constant effort. Like senior management, subordinates need to maximize the return on the assets at their disposal. Explain this concept clearly and require accountability. Remember that all companies have limited resources and that business success depends on how well assets are allocated. Cash used to pay employees is an asset that requires management!

Retaining Customers

It is far more expensive to solicit and secure new buyers of a company's products or services than it is to keep existing ones. Make sure that follow-up phone calls or visits are made to ensure customer satisfaction. Try to make 90 percent of customers happy; some will never be happy and may be more expensive and time consuming to satisfy than they are worth. Offer repeat purchase discounts. Always remember that your paycheck ultimately comes from your customers. Let them know they're appreciated.

Training Employees

Training is important. Salespeople need to know how to respond to customer concerns and up-sell other offerings as well. These skills come, in part, from education. All employees need to understand basic accounting and financial information and need to focus on profit goals. The training offerings must be efficient, however, focusing only on directly useful skills and not take people out of productivity more than necessary. This book, coupled with the Accounting In An Hour seminar, should be part of the required process.

Copying Successful Competitors

If you see that the other Laundromat, hair salon, supermarket, or hot dog stand has far more customers and seems more successful than yours, shop there. See how employees interact with customers. Look at the layout and location of the products within the store. Compare your prices to theirs. Do they have superior parking or a more highly trafficked location? Evaluate the quality of the products or services offered relative to their cost. Compliment employees and ask questions. Find out who supplies their inventory, where and how they're trained, and where they advertise. Make life easier on yourself by learning from the past mistakes of others. The business that is thriving probably made some bad decisions along the way that cost its owners money. It may have wasted resources advertising in magazines but bore fruit on billboards. There is no need to reinvent the wheel.

Selling Smart

Getting new customers costs money. Salespeople, advertising, trade shows, Internet marketing, and other means of making your product or service visible to possible buyers are a substantial line item for many companies. Make sure that the message you wish to convey is compelling and reaches the target audience. Sure, a television commercial will touch many people, but you'll be paying for the households or businesses that will never be likely customers. A trade show booth for a specific industry or targeted (legal) e-mail campaign may provide a better bang for the buck. Also, check customer credit. You don't want sales for which you'll not get paid. Writing off receivables as a bad-debt expense is painful. And the distraction of chasing deadbeats keeps you from otherwise productive activities.

Even the layout of products in a store is very important. You may notice that grocery store chains will put lower gross margin items, like milk, in the rear of the store. They may not make much money on a half gallon of the white stuff, but in order to get to the refrigerator, you must walk past many other items for which the gross margin is much higher. While waiting in line to check out, you'll be surrounded by very high (for a grocery store) gross margin items considered to be "impulse buys." Casinos are also arranged very carefully for similar reasons. The games that offer the lowest payouts per dollar are up front. To get to the more competitive games (i.e., blackjack or craps), you'll need to avoid temptation as you walk past the flashing lights of the sucker games (actually, they're all sucker games). In any case, if you own a retail establishment, do your homework to most effectively arrange the items in your store.

Try to make the best use of advertising dollars and salespeople's time. If you offer multiple products, try to consolidate ads. You may sell multiple products in a single magazine advertisement without any additional cost. Make sure that any other groups within the larger organization know what you're doing—you may be able to split the bill and save money. Similarly, a drug salesperson may work hard to get an audience at a hospital. If he or she can cross-sell other products from his or her employer, more sales may result and another division may benefit without associated payroll expenses. People who answer the phone to address customer concerns should be prepped as to how to "turn the frown upside down" and produce incremental revenue. Sell as a team. Everyone on board needs to pull whichever oar is needing a yank.

Delegating but Overseeing

You can never be everywhere. The larger one's responsibilities grow, the greater the portion of them that must be delegated. While the proverbial carrot-and-stick approach may help, there is no substitute for frequent meetings. In such encounters, lay out goals and targets and make sure they're completed satisfactorily by the next meeting. Attend a customer sales meeting to show how an effective pitch is made. Help clean the grill to show your willingness to get your hands dirty. Be a teammate, and set your folks up to win with challenging but attainable goals. Celebrate minor victories like reaching cost-cutting targets, meeting productivity goals, or landing new customers with a barbeque or bowling tournament. You don't have to spend a fortune to show appreciation.

Effective managers understand that the balance sheet is an important tool available to further company goals. We'll now describe how corporate executives might employ these methods in order to maximize shareholder value.

12

FINANCIAL STATEMENT ANALYSIS

BALANCE SHEET ANALYSIS (DOES IT LOOK OK?)

How do you tell by looking at a balance sheet if a business is doing well? The first test a company must pass is solvency. Does the company have enough cash and other liquid investments to meet its short-term needs? Generally speaking, a company should have current assets sufficient to cover its current liabilities. If this is the case, over the next 12 months, enough cash should be on hand or provided to meet upcoming needs. Of course, if the business is losing money, additional cash will be needed to support operations along with paying the existing upcoming liabilities. In addition, any necessary upcoming balance sheet modifications may also require cash. Such changes may include growth in accounts receivable, needed equipment purchases, or restocking low inventory levels.

ASSET QUALITY

Another important barometer in fiscal health determination is asset quality. A business that invested heavily in the real estate market at its peak using mostly debt (i.e., mortgages) to finance the purchases prior to a market collapse could be exposed to upcoming write-downs. Similarly, having receivables that are aging and might be susceptible to default would leave the business vulnerable, as its upcoming liabilities need to be satisfied with cash, not old customer IOUs.

One way to evaluate a company's accounts receivable quality is to look at *receivable days outstanding*. Receivable days outstanding represents how many days of sales compose aggregate accounts receivable. This may be accomplished by simply dividing the accounts receivable total on the balance sheet at the end of the year by the total revenue generated by the company on its income statement and then multiplying that ratio by 365 days. A business that has receivables of $100,000 and annual sales of $1 million would have receivable days outstanding of 36.5 days. This figure is calculated by dividing the $100,000 in accounts receivable by $1,000,000 of revenue to get 10 percent. Ten percent of a year, or 365 days, is 36.5 days. This is the average amount of time that customers take to pay the company's invoices.

If receivable days outstanding are growing and if the business a year later has to wait 50 days to get paid, a red flag might be raised. Is the company selling to creditworthy customers? Is there a risk that a significant portion of customer IOUs will default? The process of writing down or writing off these assets due to failed business counterparties might result in an expense that wipes out the entire year of earnings. Of course, the business may have seen a spike in revenue right before the end of the year, so ask detailed questions when this red flag arises.

Customers are not going to pay you more than they owe, so accounts receivable won't provide more money than their face value (as opposed to real estate, which might fetch more over time). The point here is that a company's accounts receivable are worth between 0 and 100 percent of their stated worth, never more. Watch the required collection time frame—it may give you a sense as to which end of this range is more likely.

Much like receivables, inventory generally only declines in value. In the case of Jackie's Hardware Store, Jackie's hammers might retain their value over time, but consider a 50-year-old hammer. It does not look as sophisticated as modern ones, which might be made of fiberglass instead of wood, might be lighter yet stronger, and may allow a carpenter to be more productive. A computer manufacturer's warehouse of silicon chips need to be sold quickly, as their life as cutting-edge tools is extremely short. The same holds true for grocery stores, automobile dealerships, department stores, and cellphone stores.

Food items, even cans, have expiration dates after which they may not be legally sold. Some eggs break. People order cold cuts or seafood from the counters, change their minds, and then leave the perishables on a nonrefrigerated shelf to rot. Cars that don't get sold during their model year must be heavily discounted for sale. Clothing styles and fashions change over time, even season to season, and thus lose value over time (yes, I'm forgetting about the "new" retro look). Cellular phones become obsolete almost overnight, as new features seem to become available (and suddenly necessary) every few months. In short, inventory is subject to write-downs much like accounts receivable. The management of inventory is a challenging endeavor. On one hand, it is necessary to keep some on hand to attract customers. At the same time, however, maintaining inventory is a necessary use of cash resources that are likely to decline in value. This is a reason why "just-in-time" (JIT) inventory fulfillment is attractive to many businesses. Just-in-time inventory management, as the name implies, allows companies to keep minimal amounts of goods on hand with the expectation that replacement inventory can be shipped upon short notice. Of course, just-in-time inventory controls expose the business to risk if there is a hiccup in the delivery process.

If you buy shares in a company based on the expectation that earnings (and resulting earnings per share) will grow, you might have a negative surprise when the company's annual report containing financial statements is issued. Many times, write-downs are labeled "one-time" expenses and are lumped in with nonoperating costs, even though they may be recurring on a periodic basis. Beware of companies that report "one-time" hits multiple times. Earnings per share on a Generally Accepted Accounting Principles basis is often pushed into the background while "Adjusted Earnings Per Share" (which excludes the write-down of operating assets like receivables or inventory or regular "restructuring" charges for layoffs or plant closings) are highlighted.

Generally speaking, tangible assets are much easier to finance (i.e., borrow against by using them as collateral) than intangible assets. For this reason, a business with significant tangible assets that are unencumbered (i.e., not already pledged as collateral for a loan) may have greater flexibility to borrow money or sell excess assets to generate cash in a pinch.

WATCH ACCOUNTS PAYABLE

If a business is struggling with cash flow, an early indication may be a growth in accounts payable relative to sales. In other words, if revenue is not growing (which might require more goods to be ordered), accounts payable should remain fairly flat. Companies that are feeling financial pressure still need to remain current with payroll and payroll taxes, as employees are not likely to stick around if they are not being paid on time. Banks are generally a high priority for payment, given their likely collateral position and potential for additional funding. Expenses like rent and the electricity bill are essential to remain in operation.

So if business conditions worsen and difficult choices need to be made, stretching payments to suppliers is a logical first step. Some troubled companies even switch to new suppliers that offer payment terms and avoid any payments to the old vendors to survive. Ultimately, threatened or actual litigation may result in a negotiated payment plan, but until that time comes, the company has bought breathing room. Many anxious-for-business vendors do inadequate checking of potential customers' financial strength and get burned with bad-debt expenses, which are the process of writing down accounts receivable due to payment defaults. Growth in accounts payable relative to sales is a warning sign.

A minor exception exists in the retail area, however. In anticipation of relatively high holiday sales, it is customary for stores to order disproportionately more goods at that time of year so that sufficient inventory exists to meet demand. Retailers often derive more than half of their entire annual profit in the fourth calendar quarter each year. Companies that supply retailers may show a similar but earlier trend. A sweater manufacturer might order extra wool and thread a few months prior to the prime retail season so that the sweaters are available for delivery to the retailers in advance of the holiday rush. These types of businesses may also show signs of weakness if accounts payable are growing relative to sales, but it is important to compare their balance sheets at the same point in each year.

SALE LEASEBACKS ARE RED FLAGS

As previously mentioned, sale leasebacks result in the removal of the long-term asset from a company's balance sheet. They are often executed at a discount to the market value of the assets to protect the purchaser from a short-term lease default. Selling assets cheap simultaneously with entering into an expensive lease is often a last resort, undertaken by companies on very shaky financial footing.

In September 2009, American Airlines raised $1.6 billion by selling Boeing 737 airplanes to General Electric after several consecutive quarters of net losses. These losses resulted from industry overcapacity, which forced airfares to decline as consumers increasingly used the Internet to price-shop. High oil prices, which are a significant determinant of the price of jet fuel (as much as 40 percent of airline operating expenses) also contributed to losses. American Airline's financial fortunes had seriously eroded while the easy credit environment of the 2001 to 2007 period evaporated, making one of the nation's largest airlines a sale leaseback candidate.

RETURN ON ASSETS

Much like fund managers who buy and sell stocks for investors, those who operate businesses for shareholders are evaluated based on the company's performance. One key barometer of their success (or failure) is *return on assets*. In other words, a company's management has a certain number of tools to work with, such as cash, receivables, inventory, equipment, brand names, real estate, and other assets. How much the profit the managers are able to generate using the company's asset base shows how effective a job they are doing. For example, an organization that generates $100,000 of profit through the utilization of $1 million of assets has a return on assets of 10 percent. Keep in mind that businesses in different industries often have greatly different expected returns on assets. Supermarkets, for example, provide an extremely low return on assets, while software businesses may have drastically higher asset returns. It is important for this reason to compare your company's management performance with the management of similar businesses. Executives are required to report to a company's board of directors. The board of directors is tasked with the responsibility of maximizing shareholder value (through effective asset utilization). Just as you'd like a fund manager to use managed assets (i.e., cash) to make investments that generate a high rate of return, a business operator has the same objectives, with somewhat different tools (e.g., cash, inventory, accounts receivable, and equipment).

In a very real sense, the effective management of employees is part of the process of generating a high return on company assets. After all, the use of cash for payroll has to be offset with maximum productivity. Lack of appropriate supervision leads to less-than-optimal efficiency for this significant use of resources. Employees within any business need to be in constant communication to reinforce the collective goal: making profits for the company's owners. In this fashion, workers in different divisions may be able to streamline operations. Smaller separate inventory orders may be combined in order to lower per-unit prices if people are aware of similar purchases within the organization. Shipments of varying products from vendors or to customers might be combined for transportation expense reductions. Insurance policies may be aggregated to reduce collective premiums. Multiple products might be promoted within the same advertisement at little or no incremental cost to the business as a whole.

In short, employees need to be policemen and policewomen to maximize the effectiveness of corporate assets. Arm them with the tools they need to succeed (starting with this book!). Encourage collective discussions among business units; have each group explain its operational processes. What items are selling best, and where should they be placed within a store? Which local promotions are generating the best return on investment? Share good ideas. Motivate your people to think of the company as though it were theirs. You'll be pleasantly surprised at the results.

Many moons ago, I spent a summer working as an intern for International Business Machines Corporation (IBM). My manager gave me very little to do. I was able to complete my daily tasks in about an hour! At the time, IBM was offering employees an incentive to cut costs. (I wasn't about to recommend that my job get cut, though!) Because I was about 18 years old, I thought I knew everything. After finishing my duties each morning about 10 a.m., I would spend the rest of each day walking around with a clipboard looking for inefficiencies. Any suggestions that resulted in IBM saving money provided the employee making the recommendation with 1 percent of the savings forever. And the company is huge. So, seeking my fortune, I submitted dozens of ideas ranging from moving the dumpster closer to the building to turning down the air conditioning.

None of my suggestions were implemented. But in the process, I created huge headaches for everyone else. The cost-cutting department and every division affected by my ideas had to provide written rebuttals as to why they shouldn't have to make the changes I proposed. Consequently, my efforts actually *decreased* the company's efficiency. Had my manager consolidated my superfluous position with others like mine, IBM would have saved several salaries, generated a higher return on its assets, and generated more profit for its owners, the shareholders. Plus the company would have avoided my drag on others' productivity!

RETURN ON EQUITY

Similar to the return on asset evaluation, company management performance may be graded by a *return on equity* test. This is simply the business's annual profit divided by the book equity at the beginning of the year. The primary difference between return on assets and return on equity is the fact that return on equity is a measure of asset performance *utilizing leverage*. It also shows how well the owners' equity is generating a return. If the company mentioned previously has $1 million in assets, $100,000 in annual net income also has $900,000 in liabilities, the company's equity would have a book value of $100,000 (calculated as $1,000,000 of assets minus $900,000 of liabilities). Therefore, the company's return on equity would be 100 percent (calculated as $100,000 of net income divided by $100,000 of shareholders' equity).

Return on equity demonstrates the return that is generated on the owners' capital investment in the company. The other money that is used to fund the assets of the business comes from loans. These loans, the company's liabilities, come in the form of accounts payable, debts to the Internal Revenue Service or other taxing agencies, payroll liabilities to employees, bank loans, and other obligations. Because the rate of return on equity utilizes leverage, it is expected to be much higher than the return on assets, especially when significant liabilities exist relative to shareholders' equity. The leverage may also increase return on equity's volatility more than the unleveraged return on asset evaluation. The greater the leverage, the higher the risk.

One problem that has been recently highlighted is excessive executive compensation. Dangling huge bonuses and stock options has led managers to take big risks with OPM—other people's money. When they succeed, they look like heroes, as shareholders are richly rewarded. On the other hand, failure simply means only collecting a base salary (and sometimes looking for another job). In other words, there is a strong incentive for executives to roll the dice and gamble for a big payday. This has been frequently pursued through large borrowings in order to make a reasonable return on assets result in an enormous return on equity.

LIABILITIES VERSUS EQUITY (DEBT-TO-EQUITY RATIO)

Another means of determining a company's financial safety is to look at how much it has borrowed as part of its capital structure as opposed to the amount of equity capital utilized to fund asset acquisition. The ratio of debt to equity highlights the difference between return on assets and return on equity.

Layering on debt obligations may provide a means to grow value for shareholders more quickly through faster purchase of assets, but it also increases risk. If management generates a high return on the larger asset base, shareholders may be handsomely rewarded. However, more liabilities result in higher interest rates to lenders to compensate for the augmented risk and greater ongoing debt service payments. Lower debt slows growth but provides more safety.

Of course, some companies with considerable debt-to-equity ratios over time will pay their liabilities through profits, which are added to retained earnings. In other words, a profitable company that distributes less than all of the earnings to its owners will, over time, lower its debt-to-equity ratio by replacing declining liabilities with equity in the form of increasing retained earnings. The balance sheet continues to balance.

Consider the process of buying a house by borrowing the entire purchase price in the form of a 100 percent loan-to-value mortgage. If the home value increases, all of the upside goes to the homeowner. But even with a flat home market value, regular payments will increase one's home equity, as each payment reduces the mortgage amount, which grows the equity in the house. On the other hand, the homeowner and lender may be hurt if the real estate declines in value. For example, the median home price in Detroit, Michigan, plummeted from $73,000 to $7,100 (over 90 percent) from 2006 to 2009! No, this isn't a typo. Leverage swings both ways.

AUDIT PROCESS

Are all of the liabilities properly recorded? Financial statements generally don't provide sufficient information to make this determination. For this reason, public accounting firms (like the aforementioned Big Four accounting firms for bigger businesses) are often asked to review a company's books and records to determine that the balance sheet is correct "in all material respects." Due to frequent conflicts of interest, however (such as the accounting firm having consulting contracts apart from the accounting work with the company being reviewed), some improprieties may be overlooked. In addition, a process requiring much more than spot-checking may not be realistically feasible, and unscrupulous managers are often able to mislead auditors. Once the books and records are checked by an outside accounting firm, generally done once each year, the financial results are said to be "audited." Audited results are required for public companies and provide heightened credibility for investors, lenders, vendors, and business counterparties when they are considering financial exposure to the business.

BALANCE SHEET CHANGES

Over the last year, has the business needed to add more debt to fund operations? This might suggest that the company's operations did not generate sufficient cash to fund direct and indirect costs related to operations such as inventory and payroll as well as capital expenditures like new equipment. An increase in debt is not always a bad thing, however. If a company borrows money to add new equipment due to an increase in business, the debt service is probably manageable due to the increased volume. Also, if the income statement shows heightened revenue and profit levels, a credit line used to finance receivable growth may be increased with the larger accounts receivable balance. Remember that an increase in the average age of receivables outstanding is problematic; receivables growth resulting from revenue improvement is positive. Watch receivable days outstanding.

The primary reason to be in business is to generate profits—extra money for the company's owners. Retained earnings are profits that are kept in the business. If the level of retained earnings consistently goes up from one period's balance sheet to the next, the firm is likely doing well. This buildup of equity value for shareholders may therefore become available to distribute to owners in the form of dividends. Getting paid is what it's all about!

NOTES TO FINANCIAL STATEMENTS

In addition to the numbers on a company's financial statements, an annual report will provide written descriptions of how the business is faring. The first piece of information that the notes provide is the auditor's letter that, hopefully, states that the figures contained therein are "accurate in all material respects." To the extent that the accounting firm deems the company's prospects to be dim, a qualified opinion may be provided. Such a qualified opinion letter may say that, during the audit process, it was determined that there is a risk that the business "may cease to operate as a going concern." Obviously, this kind of objective opinion by those with access to company records (likely with strong management opposition) is a huge red flag to those considering an investment, loan, or extension of credit for goods or services.

Other important information is contained in the notes to financial statements. On the balance sheet, for example, debt is classified as either short term or long term. But the notes generally provide substantial detail about when the obligations come due. For example, while all bank debt may be considered long term on the balance sheet, a painful balloon payment might be due in 13 months, just outside the short-term window. On the other hand, while you may read that a business has a certain amount of bank debt, the notes may show that there is extra availability in the company's line of credit. Such availability may enable the company to fulfill its obligations or expand operations even if there exists insufficient cash in the company's accounts to do so.

Another critical piece of information the financial statement notes provide is customer concentration. A business that relies heavily on a single buyer for its goods or services runs the risk that the primary customer chooses another vendor or defaults on its debt. Companies with many customers, none of whom make up a significant percentage of overall revenue, are much more likely to withstand a single detraction or one accounts receivable write-off.

Financial statement notes may also disclose actual or threatened litigation. Being sued is likely to distract management, resulting in less focus on operating results. Attorneys' fees are likely to increase expenses and lower profits going forward, hurting retained earnings on the balance sheet. Of course, there is always the chance that a judgment or settlement will be required at some point in the future. Sometimes, companies create an expense in anticipation of such potential future cash payments. Such an expense hits short-term earnings and sets up a liability on the balance sheet that is used as a reserve, or estimated future exposure. Beware situations where potential or real litigation is deemed by the auditors to be significant enough to warrant disclosure in a company's financial results but where the business has not provided any or insufficient reserves to provide an appropriate payoff to the plaintiffs. This would be an example of understating liabilities.

The notes generally lay out the processes that a company uses to record revenue, expense inventory, account for depreciation, prepare for contingencies, and deal with other important accounting categories. Remember that not every business, even in the same industry, uses identical methodology. A company that accelerates depreciation or expenses inventory aggressively may look less profitable than an otherwise similar competitor but might see income rise more quickly as future costs will be lower.

Even though an annual report will detail the full year's operating results and end-of-year balance sheet, there is often a section called "Subsequent Events." Included in the subsequent events portion of the notes are developments that happened after the end of the fiscal year. Positive or negative, these happenings might include a loss of a key manager, the receipt of a large customer order, or a company being approached by a buyer seeking to acquire the entire business. This is information that is more current than the financial statements. Annual reports, for example, must be released by public companies within 90 days from the end of the fiscal year; interim quarterly reports should be filed within 45 days of the end of each quarter.

Let's now take a few moments to review the material we've covered, focusing on those topics that are most important for you to retain.

13

SUMMARY AND CONCLUSIONS

I hope that you found this book to be more than the typical stereo instruction manual that finance works often mimic. A thoughtful examination should be either a solid refresher for those with significant finance and accounting experience or an eye-opener for (formerly) less sophisticated readers. It has been my goal to make people more aware of their surroundings, whether reading the business section of the newspaper, preparing for an interview, becoming a more complete and valuable employee, or just appearing smarter at one's next cocktail party.

Just like anything else, the key to financial comprehension and analysis is never to panic. Should you come across a topic or term that doesn't sound familiar, it probably can still be explained by a chapter in this book (but it may be called something a bit different). The concepts are universal.

The most important pieces of information that should be retained from this book are listed below. Read this chapter 10 times if you have to, but memorize the following:

1. An income statement shows how much money a company brings in (revenue), what it spends (costs or expenses), and what is left over (profit or loss) during a specified period of time (often a year).

2. A balance sheet displays what a company owns in the form of assets, what it owes in the form of liabilities, and what is left over for its owners in the form of net worth, or equity, at a specific point in time (often year-end). Remember the house purchase example: A $100,000 house (the asset) equals the $90,000 mortgage (the liability) plus the $10,000 down payment (the equity or net worth).

3. Current assets are expected to become (or be used as) cash within one year.

4. Long-term assets (like equipment or real estate) aren't expected to turn to cash within a year and are used to operate the business. They are initially listed on the balance sheet at their original cost.

5. Current liabilities must be paid within one year.

6. Long-term liabilities needn't be paid for at least a year.

7. The purchase of inventory is not considered an expense until the goods are sold, because the value is lost at that time. Buying an asset generally is simply the process of transferring one asset,

174

cash, into another asset and does not result in an expense as there is no immediate value loss.

8. Profitability and liquidity are not the same thing; the timing of cash receipts is often more important than paper profits.

9. Acceleration of the pace at which you account for long-term asset value decline through depreciation can increase your cash on hand.

10. A company's employees are managing the business assets for the owners. Their performance may be measured through the return generated on the assets that they oversee and the return generated on the owners' investment (equity). The cash used for payroll is one asset that must be aggressively managed for maximum productivity.

11. Provided that the balance sheets contain sufficient detail, the cash flow statement offers no new information; it just illustrates balance sheet changes.

12. Corporate scandals often result from inaccurate revenue or expense timing, misclassification of expenses through inappropriate capitalizing, or understating (or outright hiding of) liabilities.

13. Growth in accounts payable relative to sales may be an early warning sign that a business is in trouble.

14. Watch receivable days outstanding increases as an indicator that a company may not be able to collect all monies due from customers.

15. Diversification of customer base for a business provides financial stability.

16. Beware of excessive debt! It may help earnings if the extra assets acquired with the money are well managed (and generate a return in excess of the associated interest expense), but it adds significant risk and causes increased income volatility.

17. Companies have cash requirements in excess of those detailed on the income statement. Investments in equipment and facilities, or capital expenditures, keep a business competitive.

18. My 60-minute online or DVD course called Accounting In An Hour (www.AccountingInAnHour.com) explains many of these topics in a concise interactive video format. Check it out.

BALANCE SHEET (END OF LAST YEAR)

Cash	$ 100,000
Receivables	50,000
Inventory	150,000
Total Short-Term Assets	$ 300,000
Total Long-Term Assets	1,500,000
Total Assets	$1,800,000
Payables	$ 50,000
Accrued XP	50,000
Total Short-Term Liabilities	$ 100,000
Total Long-Term Liabilities	900,000
Total Liabilities	$1,000,000
Total Equity	800,000
Total Liabilities & Equity	$1,800,000

NOTES

CHAPTER 6

1. Jui Chakravorty and Kevin Krolicki, "GM Bond Deadline Passes, Bankruptcy Seen Near," *Reuters*, May 27, 2009. Available from: http://www.reuters.com/article/idUSN2651331020090527.
2. Emma Moody and Carolina Salas, "Apollo's Black Seeks Bond Swaps for Harrah's, Realogy," *Bloomberg News*, November 17, 2008. Available from: http://www.bloomberg.com/apps/news?pid=20601087&sid=aXQ3SlfgoJlc&refer=home.
3. Christopher Palmeri, "Harrah's Gets Some Debt Relief," *BusinessWeek*, April 23, 2009. Available from: http://www.businessweek.com/magazine/content/09_18/b4129027599665.htm.
4. Abigail Moses, "Auto Industry Default Risk Soars to 95% on GM, Ford," *Bloomberg News*, August, 5, 2008. Available from: http://www.bloomberg.com/apps/news?sid=aaFBEzHXsH.8&pid=20601103.

5. Douglas W. Elmendorf, *The Budget and Economic Outlook: Fiscal Years 2010 to 2020* (as presented before the U.S. Senate's Budget Committee), January 28, 2010. Available from: http://www.cbo.gov/ftpdocs/110xx/doc11014/Testimony_Frontmatter_Senate.shtml.

6. Rebecca Christie and Jody Shenn, "U.S. Treasury Ends Cap on Fannie, Freddie Lifeline for 3 Years," *Bloomberg News*, December 25, 2009. Available from: http://www.bloomberg.com/apps/news?pid=20601087&sid=abTVUSp9zbAY.

7. Jessica Holzer, "FDIC Considers Borrowing From Treasury to Shore Up Deposit Insurance," *The Wall Street Journal*, September 18, 2009. Available from: http://online.wsj.com/article/SB125328162000123101.html.

CHAPTER 7

1. Martin Wolf, "Why China's Exchange Rate Policy Concerns Us," *Financial Times*, December 8, 2009. Available from: http://www.ft.com/cms/s/0/afac7ada-e448–11de-bed0–00144feab49a.html?nclick_check=1.

CHAPTER 8

1. "Subprime Uncle Sam the FHA Makes Countrywide Financial Look Prudent," The *Wall Street Journal*, September 29, 2009. Available from: http://online.wsj.com/article/SB10001424052970204488304574428970233151130.html#articleTabs_comments%3D%26articleTabs%3Darticle.

INDEX